THE HUMAN BEING DIET

A New Way of Feasting and Fasting
for Energy, Health and Longevity
(and it will make you thinner too)

BY PETRONELLA
RAVENSHEAR

ISBN: 978-1-9993435-1-4

Dedicated with love

to my mother

Daini Teeling Smith

Contents

THE HUMAN BEING DIET

A New Way of Feasting and Fasting
for Energy, Health and Longevity
(and it will make you thinner too)

Introduction

MY VIEW ON health and nutrition has inevitably evolved since I graduated from the Institute for Optimum Nutrition. It's been shaped by my clinical practice and by the people who come to see me, and of course by lectures and books, and contact with fellow practitioners. The two modalities that have most influenced me, and the way that I practice, are clinical psychoneuroimmunology (cPNI) and Metabolic Balance™ (MB). I've worked on integrating some of the most practical aspects of both modalities into a programme that can be followed by anyone who is seeking to improve their health.

The solution to problems as diverse as low energy, inflammation and insomnia, as well as skin, digestive and weight issues is in our hands and is provided by *The Human Being Diet*. As its name implies, this is a diet that can be followed to good effect by nearly everyone excluding small children and pregnant women.

Metabolic Balance™

I was introduced to the MB programme several years ago and used it to help hundreds of people to happily reach and, more importantly, maintain their ideal weight. I first heard about the programme through my friend and colleague Gloria Parfitt, who is the MB licence holder in the UK, and I undertook the training with the programme's founder, Dr. Wolf Funfack, in 2008.

Wolf was a doctor based in Munich, who was particularly interested in nutrition. The story goes that he found himself in middle age, a little rounder than he liked, and he decided to put himself on a diet. He was disenchanted by the official advice which was that our diet should be 55% carbohydrate, 25-30% fat and 15-20% protein; he found this was of no help at all for weight loss. So he experimented by increasing the amount of protein in his diet; by trial and error he found success in eating roughly the same weight of protein to vegetable foods.

He lost weight and his patients couldn't help but notice. 'Dr. Wolf!' they cried, 'you look marvellous, what have you been doing?' The good doctor shared the details of his regime and started to devise personalised programmes for his patients; he took account of their weight loss goals, their symptoms and the results of a specialised blood test to create each programme. And his delighted patients did indeed lose weight and were much less prone to the well-known yo-yo effect, of losing weight only to put it back on again.

His premise was straightforward: give people the foods they need to bring them back to health and one of the exciting side effects is weight loss. Other benefits commonly include better sleep, less hunger, better digestion, and more energy. The MB programme was elegantly simple and Dr. Wolf prescribed it for many of his overweight and pre-diabetic patients. He had designed a programme that addressed blood sugar and insulin levels, which had a knock-on effect of balancing hormones and reducing inflammation. His patients no longer felt hungry all the time, or out of control; they lost weight and they felt great.

Dr. Wolf's MB programme provides a list of foods and a meal planner. The foods on the list can all be found in a local supermarket – there are no meal replacements, bars or shakes – just real food. Three meals are to be eaten every day, with a minimum of 5 hours between each meal; snacking is forbidden. Only water is to be drunk between meals; black tea and coffee are allowed but only with meals. The meals include one type of protein, a mixture of vegetables and, as an option, one type of fruit, but an apple a day is compulsory. And, this is the best bit, once a week a treat meal must be eaten, because pleasure is good for us too.

I used to dread it when people consulted me for weight loss because although I followed the advice we were given when I was studying nutrition, the results were very hit and miss; sometimes people lost weight and sometimes they didn't. With MB I discovered I had the best tool for helping people lose weight and keep it off. And for this I am eternally grateful to Dr. Wolf and to Gloria.

When we were training in nutrition we were taught, and to this day students are probably still being taught, that for overall health and weight loss, we must eat 3 meals and 2 snacks every day. The reasoning behind this advice was that if we go for several hours without eating, our metabolic rate (the rate at which we burn calories) drops and our weight loss plateaus.

Dr. Wolf dismissed this as nonsense. He reminded us that every time we eat, but especially when we eat carbohydrates – including grains, potatoes and sugar – the pancreas releases insulin. High carb meals and snacks increase our blood sugar and therefore our insulin, which means we're not only hungrier but fatter, as a result. Insulin is a very efficient fat-storage hormone. We are also more likely to develop all the health issues associated with 'metabolic syndrome', which include heart problems, high blood pressure and insulin resistance.

I worked with the programme for many years and consistently got great results and a long list of happy clients. MB hit the headlines when Boy George reappeared, butterfly-like, back into London life a few years ago. We were all astonished by his transformation; his before and after photos were featured in the National press. The results achieved are indeed spectacular – people really do look rejuvenated. This proves Dr. Wolf's point: <u>weight loss occurs on the programme as a</u> *side effect* of improved overall health. And it's all down to regaining control over our blood sugar and insulin.

But following the tragic death of Dr. Wolf in 2013, his programme was changed. Its simplicity was lost, and with that its appeal to me was lost too and I no longer wanted to work with it. Nevertheless, the principles of MB form the model for the perfect way to eat. The programme is available here in the UK, and worldwide, and people are still getting the same spectacular results with it (see Resources section). MB is generally offered as a package, which includes a specific blood test and private coaching sessions. It's not cheap but some coaches offer group sessions which makes it more affordable.

Psychoneuroimmunology

Leo Pruimboom, the Dutch professor who describes himself on LinkedIn as 'an evolutionary thinker, researcher and founder of clinical psychoneuroimmunology (cPNI)' is in fact a maverick genius of a scientist. He's published some fascinating papers and he's a terrific speaker. In 2011, he came to London to deliver his lecture about the pancreas – unpromising though it sounded, it was electrifying.

When I heard that he was coming to England again later that year to give his 2-year diploma course: *Clinical Psychoneuroimmunology*, I couldn't wait to sign up. Studying on Leo's course was clinically, and personally, the most valuable experience of my life. cPNI connects the dots between the mind, the nervous system and the immune system and the rest of the body. Through the lens of evolutionary biology, cPNI encompasses psychology, neurology, physiology, endocrinology, immunology (and many other –ologies including anthropology), with the aim of restoring balance, and therefore the health, of both body and mind.

cPNI teaches us that the common problems we face, problems such as obesity, skin disorders, pain, depression, insomnia, digestive disorders, frequent infections, infertility, and many others, cannot be addressed or solved in isolation. These problems need to be considered holistically; we must consider the whole person, not just the affliction. To give an example: We have a headache and we pop a painkiller. But why do we have the headache in the first place? Could it be due to dehydration? Or tension in our neck or shoulders? What's the reason for the tension that's causing the pain? We keep questioning until we find the root cause. Only then can we do something meaningful to address the problem.

cPNI and deep learning

One of the tenets of cPNI is 'deep learning'. Because if we understand the underlying causes of our maladies, we are empowered to make the changes needed to overturn them. That's why there's so much explaining in this book. If we understand the 'whys' it's much easier to make the changes. In fact, armed with this knowledge and understanding, it becomes impossible to avoid or delay making the necessary changes.

My cPNI studies with Leo and my clinical work with MB, as well as my experience of working with people to solve the problems mentioned above, inspired me to create my own programme. And the success of the programme in turn, inspired me to write this book. My aim with *The Human Being Diet* is to provide a blueprint for feasting and fasting your way to feeling, looking and being your best, whether you want to lose weight or not.

A Note on the References

References to the text are included at the end of each chapter, to prove I'm not making this up. Additional research papers, books and newspapers/magazine articles are provided for further reading. Live links, where available, have been provided for Kindle readers. In the instances where it was not possible to provide a link to the final published version of a paper in a journal (i.e. there is no access to the paper without purchasing it) a PubMed Central (PMC) link has been inserted instead.

PART 1: The Problem

1: A Brief History of Dieting, Feasting and Fasting – the diets don't work

HARDWIRED INTO OUR very DNA is the memory of our ancestors' battle to find enough food to survive. Those of us who could eat the most when food was available and those of us who were good at storing the extra food as fat survived, and survival (and reproduction of course) is success in evolutionary terms. We're programmed to eat food, and to eat as much of it as possible when we get the chance.

We've naturally got a sweet tooth because the hypothalamus in the brain equates sweetness with calories and energy, and energy equates to survival. But sugar, mainly in the form of honey, was a rare treat and involved finding both a hive and a fearless young man to climb the tree. And mostly we also like high-fat foods including butter, cheese and olive oil and we're programmed to like these foods because they are also sources of concentrated energy. It's all about survival. It goes without saying that our environment has changed beyond recognition in the last 50,000 years or so since we emerged from Africa, but our genes are pretty much the same.

Inside our 21st century body lives a very old monkey indeed. Our old monkey's successors, the cavemen, were doughty survivors. They survived hunger, thirst, extremes of temperatures and wounds from battles and wild animals – all of which had life-threatening consequences. We are the caveman survivors with the genetic memory and fear of hunger, thirst, and extreme cold or heat, written into our genes because those are the very things that killed so many of our relatives.

The spectre of starvation certainly didn't disappear in our caveman days. In the UK food rationing was introduced in 1940 and continued for 14 years – the last day of rationing was July 4th 1954, 9 years after the end of the Second World War. But in the UK we had it easy compared to many other countries. Thousands of Russians starved to death and, in Holland, the infamous Dutch Hunger Winter meant that people resorted to eating tulip bulbs and rats to survive.[1, 2] Eating for pleasure, rather than for survival, and indeed eating too much, is a relatively new indulgence in our human history.

Tribal feasting

Celebrations, religious holidays and family gatherings have always involved food. We feast our way through birthdays, weddings and bar mitzvahs and it all harks back to tribal feasting. Imagine the hunters' pride at bringing home enough food to feed the tribe – sitting round the campfire at night, listening to the stories, looking at the flickering fire, feeling safe and connected with each other and eating from the same pot. But we've lost that simple pleasure – families all over Europe and beyond hardly eat together anymore – they sit alone in front of the TV, their food on their lap. Walk through any city and food, fast food, is everywhere; billboards and burgers and people eating in the street and on the run. Food is all around us and our new survival tactic is to try and ignore it and not give in to temptation.

The diets don't work

The first ever diet book was published in London in 1863 by an undertaker called William Banting. It was called *A Letter on Corpulence* and it became a bestseller. This book was the forerunner of the Atkins type diets – carbohydrates were out but copious quantities of eggs, meat and vegetables were allowed. "Banting" became the by-word for slimming. The Banting diet was followed by Horace Fletcher's chewing diet. Fletcher said that all the ills of humankind could be solved by chewing each mouthful of food 32 times. We could eat what we liked as long as we chewed it until it was liquefied. At boarding school in 1960s England I remember the nuns trying unsuccessfully to persuade us wilful girls to adopt this practice.

Diet & Health, With Key to the Calories was published in 1919 by an overweight Californian doctor, Dr Lulu Hunt Peters; that was the first we ever heard about calories. And since then we've had endless diets including Scarsdale, Weightwatchers, Cambridge, Montignac, Atkins, Dukan, 5:2, Keto and Lighter Life with variations from low-calorie and low-fat, to high-fat-low-carbohydrate, and high-protein Paleo regimes; from powdered non-food diets to piles of red meat. All of them work but generally they don't work for long, because they are too boring, or too restrictive, or just too difficult.

When someone comes to see me for weight loss, one of my first questions is always 'What have you tried before?' And there's usually a long list of tried and failed diets which were often successful initially but later abandoned. And nearly everyone's experienced yo-yoing and has a wardrobe to prove it; it contains their perfect weight clothes, sometimes from long ago, and their 'fat' clothes. It's sometimes when there just isn't anything that fits them anymore, and they're terrified of having to buy even bigger clothes, that people come and see me.

Mindful eating i.e. thinking about what we're going to do before we do it and thinking about what we're doing when we do it, has gained popularity and has its roots in Buddhism. A combination of that and Fletcherism (relentless chewing) is recommended by the exclusive Mayr clinics in Austria. Veganism is on the rise. And we've all had enough of the food bloggers promoting the horrible idea of *Clean Eating*, which may be accompanied by a new kind of eating disorder, Orthorexia

Nervosa. Orthorexia, a term coined by Dr. Steven Bratman, denotes an obsession with 'healthy food' which can slide into an ever more restricted regime to the detriment of both physical and psychological wellbeing.

We're surrounded by food, and advertisements for food, but we don't seem to have much of an idea about what or how to eat. Perhaps part of the problem is that nowadays fewer of us sit down to eat as families. Children don't grow up eating round the table looking at what Mum and Dad eat anymore; as mentioned before, eating alone in front of the TV is the new normal. Those of us who grew up with a cosy granny making stews and apple pies and dishing out old wives' tales, such as eating carrots to help us see in the dark, are the lucky ones.

Carbohydrates are making us fatter

We've long been told that whole grains are good for us, and a vitally important part of our diet. We've also been told that we need to stick to a low-fat regime because eating fat will make us fat. But ever since we cut the fat and increased the grains, we've been getting fatter and fatter. Our weight problem is not only down to eating too much, it's also down to eating too many carbohydrates, particularly refined or high glycaemic carbohydrates – which raise blood sugar levels quickly; foods like potatoes, bread, sugar and cakes. No doubt about one thing though, we have to eat to live. But *what* and *how*, those are the questions.

To date, only one person in all the years and the hundreds of people I've coached for weight loss, had never dieted before. This lady's weight had been perfect and absolutely stable all her life until she hit menopause, when over the course of about 18 months she put on 18 pounds. She was both mystified and mortified by the weight gain, and it just kept piling on.

She'd always been fit and active and she ate pretty well. So she did more exercise and cut her food rations even further but nothing would stop this steady weight gain and she consulted me in desperation. She was beside herself. And, it has to be said, she was embarrassed, not only about the weight gain, over which she seemed to have no control, but also about having to consult me about it. She'd taken pride in her self-reliance in life, and on her sensible attitude to diet and exercise. She was embarrassed about having to ask for help and thought that I, and other people, might think that she was vain and foolish. Needless to say, this was not the case and within 10 weeks she had returned to her normal weight, and was both happy and relieved.

1   Collingham, L. 2011. The Taste of War: World War II and the Battle for Food, London, UK, Allen Lane

2   Schulz, L. C. 2010. The Dutch Hunger Winter and the developmental origins of health and disease. Proceedings of the National Academy of Sciences, 107, 16757-16758. Available: http://www.pnas.org/content/107/39/16757.full [Accessed 30 September 2018]

•   Ferguson, D. 2016. Why is America turning away from Weight Watchers? Because it's hard work [Online]. The Guardian. Available: https://www.theguardian.com/commentisfree/2016/feb/29/why-is-america-turning-away-from-weight-watchers-because-its-hard-work [Accessed 30 September 2018].

•   Press Association. 2016. Official advice on low-fat diet and cholesterol is wrong, says health charity [Online]. The Guardian. Available: https://www.theguardian.com/society/2016/may/22/official-advice-to-eat-low-fat-diet-is-wrong-says-health-charity [Accessed 30 September 2018].

2: Official Dietary Advice Needs to Change

IN THE FACE of our obesity epidemic I believe that the current UK dietary guidelines of the Eatwell Guide need to be completely revised. Dietary fat is not the enemy of weight loss, it is sugar and carbohydrates that are the problem. Encouraging us to eat cereal or toast for breakfast and to consume 33% of our daily calories as potatoes and grains sets us up for weight gain and insulin resistance, and all the concomitant problems, including heart disease.

This is the advice (page last reviewed 31/03/2017) on the NHS Eatwell website for *Starchy Foods and Carbohydrates*: '*Starchy food should make up just over a third of the food we eat. Choose higher-fibre, wholegrain varieties, such as whole wheat pasta and brown rice, or simply leave skins on potatoes. There are also higher-fibre versions of white bread and pasta. Starchy foods are a good source of energy and the main source of a range of nutrients in our diet.*'[1] That may well have been good advice decades ago, because even well into the 1960s the majority of the UK labour force were manual workers; they expended a lot of physical energy in their day[2]. We do not need to eat this kind of food when we're sitting in an office rather than toiling in a coal mine.

A rewrite of the official advice

I would suggest a total rewrite of these guidelines, perhaps something like this: '*It is recommended that the diet is based on vegetables and protein (fish, meat, eggs, poultry, and vegetarian protein sources such as lentils and beans). Healthy fats such as those found in whole foods including avocado and oily fish, as well as olive oil, are a vitally important part of the diet. Starchy and high carbo-hydrate foods, including grains, potato, sugar and fruit juice increase hunger, and encourage weight gain and insulin resistance, and should be kept to a minimum.'*

Official advice needs to change. The UK is now officially the most overweight country in Europe (as defined by a body mass index [BMI] between 25 and 30) and 27% of us are obese (BMI over 30). Hospitals may have banned super-size chocolate bars from their vending machines and the Government's 2018 sugar tax is in place, but the changes need to be much bigger than that. We are all confused about the 5-a-day rule (and it's absurd that one of the 5 a day can be fruit juice) and we're still being told that fat is bad (it's not) and that starchy carbs should make up 33% of our diet (they shouldn't).

If we continue to follow that advice, we're just going to get fatter, and more lethargic (perhaps that's the way they want us) and put an ever heavier (pardon the pun) strain on NHS resources. And by the way, we don't become fat by eating fat, we become fat because we're not burning fat, which is a consequence of our high carb diet.

The Alliance for Natural Health (ANH) has made a useful comparison of 4 recommended 'plates' on their website: http://anhinternation-al.org/2015/04/08/anh-four-plate-shoot-out/. They include the UK Government's *Eatwell Guide*, the US Government's *Choose My Plate*, the Harvard University's *Healthy Eating Plate* and their own *Food4Health* Plate. The UK's Eatwell Guide recommends substantially less protein, only 13% of daily calories, as opposed to 20-25% for the other 3 plates. It also recommends higher grain and starchy carb intake, 33%, compared with the other 3 which range between 10-24%.

If you've been following the dietary advice from either the UK or US government and you're finding it hard to lose weight, simply following the advice from Harvard or ANH, and eating more protein, is likely to help. With fewer grains and carbs and more protein, vegetables and healthy fats, you may well find that you lose weight more easily and that your energy improves too.

1   National Health Service. 2017. Starchy foods and carbohydrates [Online]. NHS. Available: https://www.nhs.uk/live-well/eat-well/starchy-foods-and-carbohydrates/ [Accessed 30 September 2018].

2   Offer, A. 2008. British Manual Workers: From Producers to Consumers, c. 1950–2000. Contemporary British History, 22, 537-571.

3: Food is Medicine – The genes load the gun, the environment pulls the trigger

THE FOOD THAT we eat speaks to our genes and alters the way they are expressed (i.e. turned on or off). This concept, of altering the way our genes are expressed, is known as epigenetics. Epigenetics can be explained with an oft used quote: *'The genes load the gun and the environment pulls the trigger'*. In other words, we are not victims of our genes. What we eat and what kind of lifestyle we have determines the way in which our genes are expressed.

The food that we eat is not just calories, protein, carbs and fats – it is received by the body as information, which communicates with our genes, turning them on and off. The genes associated with accelerated ageing, cancer and heart disease, and all the chronic diseases, are the genes that switch on inflammation inside us. We can choose to switch these genes on by eating lots of carbs and refined or fast food. Or we can silence them by eating natural, minimally processed food, which our bodies recognise as medicine.

Why do we have genes that switch on inflammation? Because inflammation is a necessary and normal part of the immune system's reaction to wounds, bacteria and danger (more about this in chapter 8). But the modern and chronic activation of the immune system, and the resultant inflammation, is not caused by wounds. It's caused by overeating, snacking, lack of sleep, sitting for long periods of time, lack of exercise and unresolved emotional stress.

Exercise is medicine too

Exercise is medicine too.[1, 2, 3] We know that it's vitally important for our physical and mental health and exercise, like food, also changes the way our genes are expressed. Bernard Jensen, the naturopath, was fond of using this quote: 'You have two doctors with you at all times, your left leg and your right leg' (but don't worry, there's no need to exercise, other than to walk, on this programme until you're ready). When we exercise, we reduce the stress hormone, cortisol, and we also increase something called brain derived neurotrophic factor (BDNF)[1]. BDNF not only makes us more intelligent, by creating new brain cells, it also helps to reduce depression and anxiety. BDNF is also increased when we fast, which is one of the reasons why exercising on an empty stomach is so good for us.

Why do we release BDNF when we're fasting and exercising? It's probably down to our old caveman survival tactics. If we were hungry (or thirsty or cold), we had to take to our feet to find the solution. And we'd better have our wits about us (hence the increased BDNF) and find what we needed, or we'd die. We didn't exercise for fun; we did it because we had to. Exercise was essential for life itself – we had to exercise to survive. Despite the massive changes in our environment and the great success with which we're ever adapting, our genes have hardly changed at all.

We've come full circle and the time has come to return to eating the foods we evolved on, the food that made us human; the food which speaks to our genes. It's time to reset our internal clocks, to restore our rhythm, to improve our gut health, to reduce the inflammation and to look after our friendly microbes. Our health depends on it – In short we need to cut out processed food, and eat more vegetables, and more fish, and to incorporate exercise into our daily life, even if it's just walking.

What we need is not a new diet, but a new way of eating, feasting and fasting, that becomes a way of life. We need a health-giving and sustainable way of eating to make us feel better; a formula which stimulates weight loss as a side effect of improved health.

1   Phillips, C. 2017. Brain-Derived Neurotrophic Factor, Depression, and Physical Activity: Making the Neuroplastic Connection. Neural Plasticity, 2017, 7260130. Available: https://www.hindawi.com/journals/np/2017/7260130/ [Accessed 30 September 2018].

2   Watters, H. 2012. Exercise Alters Epigenetics [Online]. The Scientist. Available: https://www.the-scientist.com/news-opinion/exercise-alters-epigenetics-41268 [Accessed 30 September 2018].

3   Mandolesi, L.,et al. 2018. Effects of Physical Exercise on Cognitive Functioning and Wellbeing: Biological and Psychological Benefits. Frontiers in Psychology, 9, 509. Available: https://www.frontiersin.org/articles/10.3389/fpsyg.2018.00509/full [Accessed 30 September 2018].

4: Are you Ready to Change?

THE ADVICE IN this book is not borne of clinical trials but of clinical practice; it's what I've seen working in my clinic. My clients have taught me as much as I have taught them, not only about what works but also about what's doable, and I'm so grateful to them for that. Losing weight and learning how to eat to improve our health doesn't have to be difficult or boring. There's no need for super foods or special recipes, it's just a question of eating the right quantities of foods, in the right ratios and at the right time. Making new habits is always a challenge but after the first couple of weeks of following the advice in this book you'll never look back.

Are you ready to start? Are you ready to change? Are you ready to turn your life around, to achieve and maintain vibrant health and your perfect weight?

If you're wondering how your new life will look, and wondering how changing the way you eat, and changing what you eat and when you eat, can change the way you feel, read on. You'll notice a lot of these feelings long before you've completed the 3-month programme and have moved into the forever phase. Here's a taste of what's to come:

- I wake up naturally before the alarm goes off. I feel well-rested and I'm aware that there's no pain in my body
- I drink at least ½ litre of water and prepare for my day. It feels good to start the day by doing something positively good for me
- I incorporate some morning exercise. This might be some stretching or a work-out or it might mean getting off the tube

or bus a stop or two before I need to and walking for at least 15 minutes – it feels great to move in the morning

- I'm drinking water throughout the day and only having tea or coffee with meals; I just don't need those pick-me-ups the way that I used to

- I'm not hungry between meals and the 4pm energy slump is a thing of the past

- I'm aware that my energy is better than it's ever been, my head is clear, I get much more done

- My eyes are clear and bright, my skin is rejuvenated and friends keep telling me how well I look: 'You're glowing' they tell me. And what they see on the outside is reflected by what I feel on the inside

- I feel happy in my skin; I feel happy in my clothes and that makes me feel proud of myself. I'm in control – I love the reflection in the mirror

- I feel so much better for exercising and for taking walks outdoors and I've made a point of making time for this every day

- Most evenings I've finished eating before 9pm so that my body can get on with its fat-burning and repair work while I sleep – weeknights I'm in bed by 10pm

- I've broken the habit of taking my phone or laptop to bed. Instead, I read a book and I sleep so much better for that

- My sleep is deeply refreshing and when I wake in the morning I feel enthusiastic and energised

- Once or twice a week I have a treat meal with friends. I break all the rules and feast on whatever I fancy and I know that that's good for me too

- Eating out is easy even if it's not a treat meal night. I have salad and grilled fish, meat or chicken and vegetables and it's easy to say no to dessert and to the bread basket

- My taste buds have changed. Everything tastes fresher and more alive; I don't add so much salt to my food, it just doesn't need it

- I'm not craving sugar anymore! I can hardly believe it but the idea of eating milk chocolate, biscuits, buns and cakes just doesn't appeal to me anymore. I'm free!

- On holiday I relax the rules and thoroughly enjoy myself and I also relax, happy in the knowledge that once home again, I pick up my normal way of eating and any extra pounds will melt away

- Every day I delight in the feeling of enthusiasm, lightness and energy

Doesn't that feel good? Get ready and start to feel that now; revel in the feeling of the new you. Revel in the feeling that you are not denying yourself but giving your body what it needs, like a well-oiled machine, to perform at its peak. You sleep, you exercise, you eat the foods that your body was designed to eat. Once a week you feast. You are the best that you can be.

5: Insulin and Blood Sugar

HORMONES ARE COMPLICATED and I'm sure you'll be relieved to hear that a deep dive into biochemistry is unnecessary and beyond the remit of this book. Very many hormones are involved with blood sugar and weight loss or weight gain but for simplicity the ones we're focusing on are these 4: insulin, glucagon, leptin, and ghrelin. The science might not appeal, but before we go any further it's useful to understand the basics of how insulin and these other hormones work. That phrase *'Knowledge is power'* may be hackneyed but it's true. Once we understand how dysregulated (unbalanced) blood sugar and hormones affect us, and how they affect our weight and overall health, it's easier to follow the rules of the programme. So please don't skip this part, I hope you'll find it interesting.

The orchestra

Think of our hormones, our endocrine system, as an orchestra. Every member of the orchestra is vital to the music and the harmony of the whole. To enjoy optimal health and to lose weight easily and successfully and to keep it off, we need to persuade our hormones to work together in harmony again. If one member of the orchestra is playing the wrong tune, or playing out of sync, it has a knock-on effect on everyone else and the result is not music but noise. Nothing acts in isolation in the body – when something goes wrong, when something gets out of balance, there's a cascade of hormonal activity which is designed to restore balance in a process called homeostasis. There is ongoing and constant communication between our hormones and our gut, and with our microbes, immune system and brain.

We know that insulin is a hormone and that if one hormone is out of balance it has knock-on effects on the entire hormonal system. We can take polycystic ovarian syndrome (PCOS) as an example of hormone imbalance. PCOS is linked to higher than optimal blood sugar and insulin levels and also to higher than normal testosterone levels. But the key is that the hormonal imbalance started with blood sugar and insulin imbalance (and possibly stress) and not with testosterone itself.

Sugar – friend and foe

When we eat sugar, and carbohydrates in the form of bread, biscuits, potato and cakes, our blood sugar shoots up and so does insulin. High blood sugar damages our cells; it's toxic and it's recognised by the immune system as a danger signal. In badly controlled diabetes people are at risk of losing their eyesight and limbs, and the high sugar has devastating effects on cells throughout the body, which is why insulin rises rapidly to move the sugar out of the blood and into the cells.

We know that we need sugar (glucose) for life itself. But that doesn't mean we need to eat it; the body makes the sugar that we need from the food that we eat. The easiest way for our body to make sugar is from carbohydrates, things like fruit and vegetables, grains and pulses. Sugar is stored in our liver and our muscles in the form of glycogen, so we've always got sugar in reserve which can be released into the blood when we need it.

We only have one hormone which can lower high blood sugar, and that of course is insulin. But we can raise blood sugar levels, i.e. make sugar available to fuel our brain and body in several different ways. In a process called gluconeogenesis, our body can turn proteins and fats into sugar too so that we never run out of it. Hormones such as glucagon, adrenaline, cortisol, growth hormone and thyroxine, the thyroid hormone, can all stimulate the release of sugar into the blood.

It's clear that in our evolutionary history a lack of sugar was more of a danger than too much. And now the reverse is true; we're flooding our systems with refined carbohydrates like flour and sugar and the body can't cope. When we have high insulin levels, due to eating excessive carbohydrates, we are not only hungrier but whatever we eat is likely to be stored as fat, because insulin is a fat storage hormone.

Our lifestyle is killing us

It sounds ridiculously simple but it's true to say that most of our problems arise as a direct result of overeating carbohydrates. Just to recap, the carbohydrates break down to sugar and stimulate the release of insulin. We need insulin to take the sugar to the cells – but when the cells are full of sugar they shut down their receptors. The result is too much sugar and too much insulin in the blood – simply put, this is insulin resistance. High blood sugar and high levels of insulin activate the immune system and contribute to a condition known as low-grade inflammation[1]. And low-grade inflammation is associated with all the chronic diseases referred to below – i.e. the non-communicable diseases – from heart disease to depression. For the first time in our history we are suffering and dying from lifestyle diseases rather than the ones we used to 'catch' from bacteria or viruses.

According to the WHO the non-communicable, or chronic, diseases which include metabolic syndrome (characterised by high blood pressure, overweight, high blood sugar levels and high levels of blood fats), cancer, and chronic respiratory disease, kills 41 million people a year.[2] That's 71% of deaths worldwide. *'Unhealthy diets and a lack of physical activity may show up in people as raised blood pressure, increased blood glucose, elevated blood lipids and obesity.'*

Weight loss – a side effect of improved health

We know that the weight loss occurs on this programme as a *side effect* of improved overall health. So would this be a healthy and suitable way to eat for someone who didn't want or need to lose weight? Absolutely! Some of the conditions and symptoms that could be improved on the programme, apart from metabolic syndrome, or the beginnings of Type 2 diabetes, include digestive problems such as IBS. And low energy, insomnia, PMT/PMS and PCOS, skin problems, headaches and joint pain; almost any niggling problem can be eaten away with a change of diet.

1   Minihane, A. M., et al. 2015. Low-grade inflammation, diet composition and health: current research evidence and its translation. The British Journal of Nutrition, 114(07): 999-1012. Available: https://www.cambridge.org/core/journals/british-journal-of-nutrition/article/lowgrade-inflammation-diet-composition-and-health-current-research-evidence-and-its-translation/6B2D26F3FA0E0B1D8E8BD77DA2A9F4C1/core-reader [Accessed 30 September 2018].

2   World Health Organization. 2018. Noncommunicable diseases [Online]. WHO. Available: http://www.who.int/news-room/fact-sheets/detail/noncommunicable-diseases [Accessed 30 September 2018].

•   Majid, A. 2018. Mapped: the global epidemic of 'lifestyle' disease in charts [Online]. The Telegraph. Available: https://www.telegraph.co.uk/news/0/mapped-global-epidemic-lifestyle-disease-charts/ [Accessed 30 September 2018].

•   Lustig, R. H. 2012. Fat Chance: Beating the Odds Against Sugar, Processed Food, Obesity, and Disease, New York, NY, Penguin Publishing Group

6: A Low Calorie Beginning

WE'RE NOT REMOTELY interested in counting calories on this programme – we're interested in proteins, fats and carbohydrates and getting the right ratios between them. But it must be said, the first 16 days *are* low calorie which has an energising effect on our microbes, and which in turn is good for us. But that's not the only reason why periods of calorie restriction are positively healthy. Studies have reported on the associated anti-ageing effects, as well as on blood pressure, longevity and overall health. But it's not much fun following a low-calorie diet long-term; it's boring and hard to stick to and with all the maths it can make meals a demoralising affair.

Let's consider the calorie intake of the first 16 days of the programme, which are oil and alcohol-free. The first 2 days are vegetables only and very low in calories; during the next 14 days, you'll still only be consuming between 800 and 900 calories a day. Once you add the daily 3 tablespoons of oil, you'll be taking in around a total of 1220-1300 calories a day. That means you *are* on a low-calorie diet, with all the benefits the studies have shown, and without ever having to count one. You're eating whole fresh foods and every single calorie you're eating is giving you great nutrition in return. But the key to sustaining this diet lies in the weekly treat meal from day 17 onwards; breaking all the rules and feasting makes the programme easier, possible even, to stick to.

Several research studies point to the health-giving and anti-ageing effects of restricting calories.[1,2,3] A study carried out in 2015 on overweight individuals showed that a low-calorie diet increased levels of friendly gut bacteria. After just one week on a low-calorie diet levels of Lactobacilli species and Akkermansia muciniphila had increased. Akkermansia is inversely associated with obesity, diabetes, and cardio-metabolic diseases and low-grade inflammation and it sticks to, and strengthens, the lining of the digestive tract. It is a fascinating microbe which, to nourish itself, eats away at the mucus lining the gut, in essence helpfully pruning the gut lining which makes it more resilient,[4,5,6] but Akkermansia is only active when we're fasting.

1   Nicoll, R. & Henein, M. Y. 2018. Caloric Restriction and Its Effect on Blood Pressure, Heart Rate Variability and Arterial Stiffness and Dilatation: A Review of the Evidence. International Journal of Molecular Sciences, 19(3):751. Available: https://www.mdpi.com/1422-0067/19/3/751/htm [Accessed 30 September 2018].

2   Redman, L. M. et al 2018. Metabolic Slowing and Reduced Oxidative Damage with Sustained Caloric Restriction Support the Rate of Living and Oxidative Damage Theories of Aging. Cell Metabolism, 27(4):805-815.

3   Ott, B. et al., 2017. Effect of caloric restriction on gut permeability, inflammation markers, and fecal microbiota in obese women. Scientific Reports, 7, 1-10. Available: https://www.nature.com/articles/s41598-017-12109-9 [Accessed 30 September 2018].

4   Reunanen, J. et al 2015. Akkermansia muciniphila Adheres to Enterocytes and Strengthens the Integrity of the Epithelial Cell Layer. Applied and Environmental Microbiology, 81(11):3655-3662.Available: https://aem.asm.org/content/81/11/3655 [Accessed 30 September 2018].

5   Remely, M. et al 2015. Increased gut microbiota diversity and abundance of Faecalibacterium prausnitzii and Akkermansia after fasting: a pilot study. Wiener Klinische Wochenschrift, 127(9-10):394-8 Available: https://link.springer.com/article/10.1007%2Fs00508-015-0755-1 [Accessed 30 September 2018].

6   Cani, P., De Vos, M., 2017. Next-Generation Beneficial Microbes: The Case of Akkermansia muciniphila. Frontiers in Microbiology, (8)1765. Available: https://www.frontiersin.org/articles/10.3389/fmicb.2017.01765/full/ [Accessed 30 September 2018].

7: Leptin (and Ghrelin, the Hunger Hormone)

AS WELL AS insulin and glucagon, we need to mention 2 other hormones which can regulate our appetite, and our ability to lose or gain weight: leptin, which wasn't discovered until 1994, and ghrelin, discovered in 1999. Leptin is the satiety or 'fullness' hormone and ghrelin is the hunger hormone. As long as everything is working as it should in our body, leptin, which is produced by our fat cells, acts as a satiety signal, i.e. it should say to us 'I've had enough to eat, I can stop now, I've got enough energy'.

Our fat cells communicate with the brain via leptin and let it know how much energy is available. Leptin tells the brain that there's enough spare energy for us to be able to reproduce and to have fun. Or it says there isn't enough energy in which case our brain will drive us to find food. Leptin resistance means we never feel full – we can always eat more.

Leptin resistance

We can become leptin-resistant when we're carrying too much fat, especially around the middle, and as a result, we can't stop eating. The brain is getting the message 'I'm starving, I haven't got enough energy and I need to eat'. Normally we stop eating when we're full, but if we're overweight and leptin-resistant we only stop eating when there is nothing left to eat. Leptin resistance is still a controversial subject – some say that it's preceded by insulin resistance and some say it's the other way around – either way, we don't want it – leptin and insulin resistance are the precursors of disease.

So whereas leptin is the 'I'm full' hormone when it's working as it should, ghrelin is the 'I'm hungry' hormone. Ghrelin is made in our stomach when it's empty. And like leptin, ghrelin gets into the blood stream and crosses the blood-brain barrier, and says to the hypothalamus 'I need food'. Most of us have experienced feeling particularly hungry when we haven't slept enough and that's because ghrelin is increased, and leptin is decreased, when we're sleep deprived.[1] But there's an easy way to hijack the hunger signal from ghrelin – have a big glass (a pint/half a litre) of water to stretch out your stomach and ghrelin slinks away.

The neurosurgeon turned health advocate, Dr. Jack Kruse,[2] reversed his poor health by overcoming his own leptin resistance and he lost more than 130lbs (over 9 stone) in a year. He tells us that the reason Oprah, whose yo-yo weight struggle is known to all, is still overweight is because she's leptin resistant. For Oprah and all of us who are leptin resistant, he recommends a breakfast of at least 50g protein within 30 minutes of waking. He says we must eliminate snacks, eat 3 meals a day, and limit our carb intake to below 50 grams per day for 6-8 weeks. That's pretty much what we are going to be doing on this programme. We are going to bring our hormones to heel and get hunger and blood sugar under control, and feel better and brighter every day.

Middle-aged spread

I'm going to tell you a personal story because I think it helps to illustrate the leptin resistance/weight problem well. Almost overnight (obviously not overnight but it was certainly quick) I was catapulted into menopause. My weight shot up from 54kg to 63kg (9 kilos is nearly 20 pounds or 1.4 stone). Not only that but I was having a hellish time with hot flushes and insomnia and I thought, if this is the way it's going to be I don't want to be here anymore; I was seriously depressed.

I nastily thought that people exaggerated about their menopausal symptoms, and this was a good albeit brutal lesson for me. Some women suffer not only weight gain but also anxiety, insomnia, mood swings and depression, as well as awful sweats, whereas others just sail through it. I found that although I was always hungry, it didn't matter how hard I tried or how little I ate, the weight kept piling on. Eventually I gave in and went on bioidentical hormone replacement therapy (BHRT) and that really helped. The sweats, anxiety and insomnia receded but although I stopped gaining weight I still couldn't lose it.

It began to dawn on me, no thanks to the hormone imbalance and my dozy brain, that I had become insulin and leptin resistant. I was in a state of low-grade inflammation and had the depression to prove it. What I'd always done was no longer working; my body and my hormones had changed and I realised that I had to change too. I had to get the rhythm back into my life (see the Resetting our Rhythm chapter). Having avoided breakfast throughout my adult life, I made myself eat protein for breakfast. I stopped looking at my phone after 8pm, I went to bed earlier, I took myself out for walks before meals. And within a couple of months I was back in balance and had lost the weight. And the depression.

1   Shostak, A., Husse, J., Oster H. 2013. Circadian regulation of adipose function. Adipocyte 2(4): 201 206.Available: https://www.ncbi.nlm.nih.gov/pmc/articles/PMC3774695/#R59 Final version (Abstract): https://www.tandfonline.com/doi/abs/10.4161/adip.26007 [Accessed 30 September 2018]

2   Kruse, J. (2011). *Why is Oprah still Obese?.* [online] Jackkruse.com. Available at: https://jackkruse.com/why-is-oprah-still-obese-leptin-part-3/ [Accessed 10 Oct. 2018].

•   Richards, B. J. & Richards, M. G. 2009. Mastering Leptin, Your Guide to Permanent Weight Loss and Optimum Health Minneapolis, MN, Wellness Resources Books.

•   Kruse, J., 2013. Epi-paleo Rx: The Prescription for Disease Reversal and Optimal Health. Optimized Life PLC

•   Rettberg, J. R., Yao, J. & Brinton, R. D. 2014. Estrogen: A master regulator of bioenergetic systems in the brain and body. Frontiers in Neuroendocrinology, 35(1):8-30. Available: https://www.ncbi.nlm.nih.gov/pmc/articles/PMC4024050/ [Accessed 30 September 2018]

•   Wang, T. et al. 2013. Relationships between changes in leptin and insulin resistance levels in obese individuals following weight loss. Journal of Medical Sciences.

29(8):436-443. Available: https://www.sciencedirect.com/science/article/pii/S1607551X12003622 [Accessed 30 September 2018].

- Stern, J., Rutkowski J., Scherer, P. 2016. Adiponectin, Leptin, and Fatty Acids in the Maintenance of Metabolic Homeostasis through Adipose Tissue Cross talk. Cell Metabolism 23(5):770-784. Available: https://www.cell.com/cell-metabolism/fulltext/S1550-4131(16)30162-0 [Accessed 10 October 2018]]

8: Danger Signals and Low-Grade Inflammation

ALL OUR CHRONIC diseases, including depression, obesity, allergies, heart diseases, type 2 diabetes, auto-immune diseases, migraine, osteoporosis, asthma, and skin problems including dermatitis, acne and eczema, share a common underlying condition. That condition is inflammation. This isn't a new discovery; researchers first identified higher levels of inflammation in people with type 2 diabetes in the 1950s.[1] Inflammation affects our brain too and can make us depressed or anxious.[2]

We can see external inflammation; the redness and swelling of an insect bite, the swelling of a twisted ankle, a skin rash; inflammation is characterised by heat, redness, swelling and pain. But what about the inflammation on the inside, the invisible inflammation, how is that manifested? If you have any of the conditions mentioned above and especially if anything hurts, you can be sure that you're in a state of low-grade inflammation. Low-grade inflammation means that the immune system has been activated and left to rumble on without being switched off again. And that's when chronic disease starts. But where did the inflammation come from in the first place? And why hasn't the immune system switched it off?

Danger signals activate the immune system

Danger signals in our body, such as high blood sugar and insulin, can also arise from environmental toxins and chemicals, mould and bacteria, processed foods, emotional stress, excessive exercise and even sitting down for too long. All these danger signals are stressors, which activate our immune system. Immune system activation and inflammation go hand in hand because the immune system triggers inflammation as a normal part of the healing process. Inflammation is the first step the immune system takes to resolve wounds and infections.

But our modern lifestyle diseases and maladies are nothing to do with wounds and infections. These diseases occur because of what and how we eat, how we exercise and how we sleep, and how we deal with stress.

Loneliness is dangerous too

Another internal danger signal, and therefore another risk factor for inflammation and disease, is isolation and loneliness. Humans, like most mammals, are designed for life in a community. Julianne Holt-Lunstad, at Brigham Young University, looked at 218 studies involving nearly 4 million people to investigate the effects of loneliness on our health.[3] The first sentence in her paper reads: '*Our social relationships are widely considered crucial to emotional well-being; however, the possibility that social connection may be a biological need, vital to physical well-being and even survival, is commonly unrecognized*'.

Holt-Lunstad's analysis of all the studies revealed that people with a good social network were 50% less likely to die prematurely. So now we know, we have scientific evidence to prove that loneliness is bad for us. Getting out of the house or out of the office and spending more time with family and friends and widening our social circle, makes us healthier.

Our genes, which haven't changed much over the past 50,000 years, and our immune system evolved and allowed us to adapt to a life outdoors in the fresh air, exercising as part of our daily life; we lived in harmony with the 24-hour circadian (circa: around and dian: day) rhythm of the day. Our immune system learnt to deal with infections and wounds and short sharp shocks. It doesn't understand physical inactivity (look up *'sedentary death syndrome'*[4] on the internet), chronic overeating and snacking, chronic sugar consumption, chronic stress such as mortgages, chronic exposure to artificial light and chronic sleep deprivation.[5]

Our body responds to all these stressors with inflammation; that's all it's got. There's nothing in the artillery of our ancient immune system that can be used to combat the effects of our modern lifestyle.

1   De Luca, C. & Olefsky, J. M. 2007. Inflammation and Insulin Resistance. FEBS letters, 582(1):97-105. Available: https://febs.onlinelibrary.wiley.com/doi/full/10.1016/j.febslet.2007.11.057 [Accessed 30 September 2018].

2   Raison, C. L., Capuron, L. & Miller, A. H. 2006. Cytokines sing the blues: inflammation and the pathogenesis of depression. Trends in Immunology, 27(1):24-31. Available: https://www.ncbi.nlm.nih.gov/pmc/articles/PMC3392963/ [Accessed 30 September 2018].

3   Holt-Lunstad, J. 2017. The Potential Public Health Relevance of Social Isolation and Loneliness: Prevalence, Epidemiology, and Risk Factors. Public Policy & Aging Report, 27(4):127-130. Available: https://academic.oup.com/ppar/article/27/4/127/4782506 [Accessed 30 September 2018].

4   Lees, S. J. & Booth, F. W. 2004. Sedentary death syndrome. Canadian Journal of Applied Physiology, 29, 447-460.

5   Bosma-Den Boer, M. M., Van Wetten, M.-L. & Pruimboom, L. 2012. Chronic inflammatory diseases are stimulated by current lifestyle: how diet, stress levels and medication prevent our body from recovering. Nutrition & Metabolism, 9(1):32. Available: https://nutritionandmetabolism.biomedcentral.com/articles/10.1186/1743-7075-9-32 [Accessed September 30 2018]

•   Chen, L., Chen, R., Wang, H. & Liang, F. 2015. Mechanisms Linking Inflammation to Insulin Resistance. International Journal of Endocrinology, 2015, 1-9. Available: https://www.hindawi.com/journals/ije/2015/508409/ [Accessed 30 September 2018].

•   Methodist Hospital Houston. 2013. *Obesity makes fat cells act like they're infected* [Online]. Science Daily. Available: https://www.sciencedaily.com/releases/2013/03/130305145145.htm [Accessed 30 September 2018].

•   Sears, B. & Perry, M. 2015. The role of fatty acids in insulin resistance. *Lipids in Health and Disease,* 14(1). Available: https://lipidworld.biomedcentral.com/articles/10.1186/s12944-015-0123-1 [Accessed 30 September 2018].

9: Digestion and Leaky gut

WHEN WE'RE TALKING about our general health we also need to talk about the gut. And this is so important that the gut, and gut health, gets a chapter all to itself. By 'gut' I'm not referring to a paunch or belly but rather to the digestive system, including the stomach, small intestine and large intestine. Our gut is like a hosepipe running through the body, from mouth to anus; an internal hosepipe surrounded by blood vessels and the rest of the body. It's our interface with the outside world and that's why 70-80% of the immune system is found here. We don't want any bugs sneaking into the rest of the body via the gut.

The Victorians knew that chewing our food properly was good for us – they worked out that saliva contains protein, fat and carbohydrate digesting enzymes. Later, thanks to Alexander Fleming, we discovered that it contains lysozyme, also found in our tears and elsewhere, which is a mild antibacterial. But even before we start chewing, with just the anticipation of eating, with only the thought of food or the sight or smell of it, the stomach starts secreting stomach acid (hydrochloric acid/HCl) and the pancreas starts mixing up a cocktail of enzymes ready to digest whatever's coming its way.

HCl is vital stuff; it doesn't matter how good our diet is, if we can't digest and absorb the foods that we're eating we might as well eat rocks. We need B vitamins and zinc to make HCl, but if we haven't got HCl in the first place, we're not absorbing the Bs and the zinc, and we can't make it. It's a vicious cycle. The good news is that we can supplement with Betaine HCl and, in my view, it's the most important supplement of all and I recommend it to practically everyone who comes to see me. HCl levels fall with age, with zinc deficiency (very common) and of course with the use of antacids, over the counter or prescription. If you're working out but you can't seem to build muscle, HCl can help, by transforming the protein that you eat into your muscles. But it mustn't be taken if you suspect, or know, that you have stomach ulcers.

Sex, zinc and acid

By the way, one of the reasons so many of us are zinc deficient is because of our high carb diet – remember that carbs break down to sugar and stimulate insulin secretion? We need zinc for the synthesis, storage and secretion of insulin so eating those carbs drains our zinc stores.[1,2] But we also need zinc for a healthy immune system and for wound healing and healthy skin. And men, you need it for fertility and for semen production[3] – every time you ejaculate you're getting rid of your zinc.

Zinc is needed to make testosterone and also for a healthy libido and the oyster's reputation as an aphrodisiac might be due to the high quantity of zinc it contains. Some signs of zinc deficiency include poor sense of taste or smell, white spots on the fingernails and stretch marks.

One of the main enemies of stomach acid production is stress. Imagine you leave a restaurant and you see a tiger. Do you say to him 'Well I *would* run away, but I need to digest my lunch first'? No of course not; we don't stop to think, we take to our heels and run. That fight or flight response, which is our reaction to any kind of stress, means that digestion is put on hold. We're not going to be digesting anything if we're running or fighting for our life. What happens next is that rather than being digested and absorbed, the food sits in our gut and starts to ferment. And with fermentation comes bloating and burping and sometimes reflux and HCl can help to overcome these problems.

So we chew our food and swallow it and it arrives in the stomach. The stomach's highly acidic environment is designed to kill any bugs coming in and this is where protein digestion begins. Then the food, churned up and covered in stomach acid, heads into the small intestine which is where the digestive enzymes get to work; this is where most of our digestion and absorption takes place. Then on to the colon – home to the biggest collection of our amazing microbes – and finally out the other end. The whole process takes anything from about 48-72 hours.

The gut is not Las Vegas

Complementary practitioners have long warned about 'leaky gut' or 'intestinal permeability' as it's formally known. And that idea was long derided by medics but in 2000, the brilliant Italian scientist Alessio Fasano and his research team made a breakthrough – they discovered a protein called zonulin in the lining of the gut. And they found that when higher than normal levels of zonulin were present, the result was a leaky gut.

This discovery led to Fasano's famous quote: *'The gut is not like Las Vegas. What happens in the gut does not stay in the gut'*. His seminal paper was published in 2012, *Intestinal Permeability and its Regulation by Zonulin: diagnostic and therapeutic implications*.[4] There's a link to the full text below and it's well worth reading. Fasano likens the gut to a battlefield where everything that comes into it must be correctly, and crucially important-ly, recognised as friend or foe.

The cells in the lining of the gut are held together by 'tight junctions'. We used to believe that the tight junctions remained 'tight', i.e. they couldn't open and were cemented together. Up until Fasano published his research we thought that the only way substances could move from the gut to the blood stream was by passing through the cells' membranes themselves. But now we know that these tight junctions are more like doors between the cells; they allow substances to escape through the gut lining and into the body. Zonulin is the protein that's in charge of opening the doors between the cells; it's the gatekeeper between the gut and the rest of the body.

Leaky gut & autoimmune disease

Fasano initially discovered in the early 2000s that his celiac patients were prone to leaky gut and he later worked out that this was because they were producing too much zonulin. He went on to discover that many auto-immune diseases, including rheumatoid arthritis, inflammatory bowel disease and type 1 diabetes all share 3 common denominators, inflammation, zonulin and leaky gut.

So now we know. A leaky gut sets the scene for allergies, auto-immune diseases, musculoskeletal pain, skin problems including psoriasis and acne, low energy and depression, and much else besides. We learned earlier that lifestyle diseases are now the commonest cause of death and disability, and that they are linked to chronic inflammation. And it seems that one of the commonest causes of chronic inflammation (alongside the other 'danger' signals like high insulin and blood sugar, physical inactivity and dysregulated hormones) is a leaky gut, because a leaky gut, like all those other danger signals, activates the immune system. Leaky gut affects us in absolutely every way, from how we feel, to how we look, to how we function.

It's odd to think that even if we don't have any obviously gut related symptoms such as IBS, bloating or heartburn we can still have a leaky gut – in fact, due to our daily stress and diet and lifestyle, we can take it as read that we all have it. Nobody knows for sure what zonulin is for – this is science hot off the press. But because there's only one food known to man which increases zonulin (we'll come to that later) and because we know zonulin increases in response to the wrong kind of bacteria in the gut, maybe it's a way of alerting the immune system to danger.

Leaky gut attracts the immune system

What's the problem with leaky gut? Imagine a sieve with all its holes – when the gut's leaky not only do undigested, or partly digested, proteins escape into the blood stream, but so also do bacteria and any other pathogens and toxins that happen to be hanging about.[5] When the immune system comes across what it perceives as a foreign invader, i.e. anything that's not 'self', it goes into full attack mode. That's one of its primary jobs, to recognise self from non-self. Like a Rottweiler, it doesn't pause for thought, it's all systems go. Bacteria, which of course our immune system is geared up to attack, multiply very fast so the lightning speed of the immune response is vitally important.

To recap: immune system activation results in inflammation – when our immune system is constantly activated by a leaky gut, the result is a chronic state of low-grade inflammation, and increased susceptibility to auto-immune disease.[6]

1   Supplements, 2018. Zinc [Online]. ODS. Available: https://ods.od.nih.gov/factsheets/Zinc-HealthProfessional/ [Accessed 30 September 2018].

2   Fukunaka, A. & Fujitani, Y. 2018. Role of Zinc Homeostasis in the Pathogenesis of Diabetes and Obesity. International Journal of Molecular Sciences, 19(2):476. Available: https://www.mdpi.com/1422-0067/19/2/476/htm [Accessed 30 September 2018].

3   Fallah, A., Mohammad-Hasani, A. & Colagar, A. H. 2018. Zinc is an Essential Element for Male Fertility: A Review of Zn Roles in Men's Health, Germination, Sperm Quality, and Fertilization. Journal of Reproduction & Infertility, 19(2)69-81. https://www.ncbi.nlm.nih.gov/pmc/articles/PMC6010824/ [Accessed 30 September 2018].

4   Fasano, A. 2012. Intestinal Permeability and Its Regulation by Zonulin: Diagnostic and Therapeutic Implications. Clinical Gastroenterology and Hepatology, 10(10):1096-1100. Available: https://www.cghjournal.org/article/S1542-3565(12)00932-9/fulltext [Accessed 30 September 2018].

5   de Punder, K. and Pruimboom, L. 2015. Stress Induces Endotoxemia and Low-Grade Inflammation by Increasing Barrier Permeability. Frontiers in Immunology, (6):223. Available: https://www.frontiersin.org/articles/10.3389/fimmu.2015.00223/full [Accessed 10 October 2018]

6   Sturgeon, C. & Fasano, A. 2016. Zonulin, a regulator of epithelial and endothelial barrier functions, and its involvement in chronic inflammatory diseases. *Tissue Barriers,* 4(4): e1251384. Available: https://www.tandfonline.com/doi/full/10.1080/21688370.2016.1251384 [Accessed 30 September 2018].

•   Campos, M. 2017. Leaky gut: What is it, and what does it mean for you? [Online]. Hardvard Health Publishing. Available: **https://www.health.harvard.edu/blog/leaky-gut-what-is-it-and-what-does-it-mean-for-you-2017092212451** [Accessed 30 September 2018].

10: What Makes the Gut Leaky?

STRESS, **EXCESSIVE ALCOHOL,**[1] excessive exercise (athletes are a case in point),[2,3] lack of exercise, bacterial or fungal overgrowth, overeating, lack of commensal (good) bacteria, and nutrient deficiencies including vitamins A and D and zinc, can all result in a leaky gut. And so can the standard Western diet – termed SAD (standard American diet) in the U.S. - which is comprised of refined and processed food and too much sugar and fructose (from fruit, fruit juice and high fructose corn syrup). Even lack of sleep is bad for our gut health[1].

Gluten and zonulin

But there's one more thing to add to that list. Of all the foods we eat, and of all the different proteins, there is one protein that is indigestible to human beings. That protein, found in wheat, rye and barley, is gluten. It's not only indigestible but it also increases zonulin, which as we know makes the gut leaky. Undigested gluten attracts the immune system and Fasano says, '*I am now convinced that our immune system mistakenly interprets gluten as a component of a dangerous bacterium or bacteria*'.[4]

I met Fasano (who is as personable as he is brilliant) when he came over to lecture in London at the CAM conference 'Meeting the Microbiome' in 2015, and I asked him if he ever ate gluten. '*No*' he replied, '*not very often*' he added. Not a very interesting question I know, but it was early in the morning. He's currently running stage 3 trials on a drug, Larazotide acetate, which inhibits zonulin release, for those with auto-immune diseases including celiac disease.

When I first cut gluten out of my diet I became more sensitive to it and if I inadvertently ate some at a restaurant, the next day I felt hungover and fuzzy-headed. Research is ongoing into 'Non-celiac Gluten Sensitivity' (NCGS)[5] because it seems that more and more people who are not celiac are reacting to either gluten or wheat, or both. Neurologists, including David Perlmutter, author of *Grain Brain,* are now saying that the number one organ affected by gluten in non-celiacs is not the gut, but the brain.

So that's why there's so much noise about wheat. A few people seem to be able to get away with eating it – even testing wheat after 2 weeks without it (see below) doesn't give them any grief. But celiacs can't eat any gluten foods; some are sensitive to the tiniest crumb and will suffer instant pain, vomiting or diarrhoea. Gluten-containing bread, pizza, croissants, croutons and cake are off the menu forever for them.

Fuzzy-headed

Part of a homework assignment, when I was studying nutrition, was to strictly avoid wheat for 2 weeks. We thought that would be easy but it turned out that wheat was everywhere, and in the most unlikely places; we found it in liquorice sweets, taramasalata and sausages. At the end of the 2 weeks we were to have 2 Weetabix on an empty stomach and report back. Every single person in our group experienced unpleasant symptoms of one kind or another. Some of us felt very tired, and a feeling of 'brain-fog' was common. Some also experienced skin break outs, food cravings, joint pain, anxiety, as well as gut problems like bloating and pain, and constipation or diarrhoea.

Personally speaking I felt so depressed I could hardly drag myself out of bed the next day. I had no idea that wheat was having any effect on me. After about 3 months of being wheat-free I noticed another effect. One morning I was applying concealer to the dark circles under my eyes, as usual, when I noticed that the black bags were gone and I've never used concealer since (or gone back to eating wheat).

For non-celiacs, me included, who'd rather not have a leaky gut and a fuzzy head, and who'd rather decrease than increase their chances of getting an auto-immune disease, avoiding gluten is a no-brainer. This programme is all about improving health and that's why there's no wheat, and no rye or barley initially. You can do the wheat experiment yourself – do without gluten absolutely 100% for at least 2 weeks and then try some rye bread. See what happens and see how you feel over the next couple of days. A few days later you can try the same thing with wheat bread.

Of all the factors contributing to leaky gut, most of them are easy to avoid: we can choose not to eat gluten, we can (unless we're alcoholics) drink in moderation, we can limit excessive exercise (unless we're athletes) and at the same time remain physically active. We can eliminate bacterial or fungal overgrowth (see the candida section) and we can eat a wide variety of whole foods including vegetables to feed our good bacteria. We can avoid eating processed meat, too many calories and carbs and too much fructose, and we can ensure good levels of vitamins A and D and zinc, via diet and supplements. And we can go to bed earlier and sleep for longer.

Stress and exercise and leaky gut

Remember we respond to any kind of stress with fight or flight - which switches off digestion, and everything else that's not needed for our immediate survival - but why does it make the gut leaky? Stressors, whether they be psychological (e.g. traffic wardens/ mortgages/ deadlines) or physiological (e.g. extreme exercise/trauma) trigger a cascade of hormones that produces immediate changes in our body. Our heart starts racing, our muscles tense up, our breathing quickens and we might also break into a sweat.

Those are some of the physical fight or flight effects which result from the activation of the sympathetic nervous system (SNS), which in turn activates the hypothalamic-pituitary-adrenal (HPA) system. These stress systems release adrenalin, noradrenalin and cortisol, together with inflammatory chemicals. The result is immune system dysregulation, gut microbe alteration, leaky gut and inflammation. That's why athletes, including marathon runners, suffer not only with leaky gut but also with higher rates of respiratory infections post competition. Any kind of stress automatically results in a leaky gut. To combat stress, we can change the way we eat, and change the way we sleep and change the way we exercise; those changes will, in turn, help to prevent a leaky gut and get the inflammation under control.

Psycho-emotional stress

Psychological stress is possibly the trickiest health risk to address, and it's vitally important that we do. We can meditate and use Apps like Headspace to help us, we can write about our feelings and process them that way. We can get more sleep. We can take up yoga or Tai Chi. We can talk to friends. We can use cPNI or Rapid Transformational Therapy (RTT) – see the Resources section - to help us understand and process the traumatic events of the past that are still affecting us, by chronically activating our HPA response, today.

1   Swanson, G. R. et al 2015. Decreased melatonin secretion is associated with increased intestinal permeability and marker of endotoxemia in alcoholics. American Journal of Physiology - Gastrointestinal and Liver Physiology, 308(12):G1004-G1011. Available: https://www.physiology.org/doi/full/10.1152/ajpgi.00002.2015 [Accessed 10 October 2018]

2   Karhu, E., Forsgård, R., Alanko, L., Alfthan, H., Pussinen, P., Hämäläinen, E. and Korpela, R. 2017. Exercise and gastrointestinal symptoms: running-induced changes in intestinal permeability and markers of gastrointestinal function in asymptomatic and symptomatic runners. European Journal of Applied Physiology, 117(12):2519-2526.

3   Mach, N. and Fuster-Botella, D. 2016. Endurance exercise and gut microbiota: A review. Journal of Sport and Health Science, 6(2):179-197. Available: https://www.sciencedirect.com/science/article/pii/S2095254616300163 [Accessed 10 October 2018]
Available: https://link.springer.com/article/10.1007%2Fs00421-017-3739-1 [Accessed 10 October 2018]

4   Fasano, A., Flaherty, S. & Gannon, R. 2014. Gluten Freedom: The Nation's Leading Expert Offers the Essential Guide to a Healthy, Gluten-Free Lifestyle, Toronto, CA, John Wiley & Sons Canada, Limited.

5   Losurdo, G. et al 2018. Extra-intestinal manifestations of non-celiac gluten sensitivity: An expanding paradigm. World Journal of Gastroenterology, 24(14):1521-1530. Available: https://www.wjgnet.com/1007-9327/full/v24/i14/1521.htm [Accessed 10 October 2018]

•   Perlmutter, D., 2013. Grain Brain, New York, NY, Little Brown & Company.

•   Bischoff, S. C., Barbara, G., Buurman, W., Ockhuizen, T., Schulzke, J.-D., Serino, M., Tilg, H., Watson, A. & Wells, J. M. 2014. Intestinal permeability – a new target for disease prevention and therapy. BMC Gastroenterology, 14(1) 189. Available: https://bmcgastroenterol.biomedcentral.com/articles/10.1186/s12876-014-0189-7 [Accessed 10 October 2018]

11: Our Old Friends

OUR **'OLD FRIENDS'** is the term, coined by Graham Rook of University College London, for our friendly microbes. As he points out: '*We are not individuals. We are ecosystems with microbial partners (microbiota) that are involved in the development (particularly in early life) and function of essentially every organ, including the brain. In fact we have more microbes in our guts than we have human cells in our bodies, and vastly more microbial DNA and genes than human genes.*'[1]

Microbes play a vitally important part in our physical and emotional health and as Rob Knight writes: '*It's a common personal experience that changing your diet can change your mood. Because changing your diet also changes your microbes, it's entirely possible that some of these effects have a microbial component. And if microbes can change our health and our minds, the next question is can we change our microbes to improve ourselves?*'[2]

We are only as healthy as our microbes

It's finally dawned on us that we are only as healthy as our microbes. You've probably heard that we are only 10% human – we are made up of some 10 trillion human cells and about 100 trillion microbial cells. Human beings have about 20,000 genes compared to the 2 million to 20 million microbial genes. Our own DNA pales into insignificance when we consider the numbers and the impact of the microbial DNA.

The things you'll be doing on this programme are good for your health because they're good for *their* health. Here are just a few examples of what these creatures do for us: they make the lining of the gut more resilient, they communicate with the immune and nervous systems, they make vitamins for us and they make substances which energise the liver and the gut itself. They even affect our mood. Some of my favourite microbe books include: *Follow Your Gut (2015)* by Rob Knight, *The Psychobiotic Revolution (2017)* by Scott Anderson and *Missing Microbes (2014)* by Martin Blaser. All of these books are fascinating and refreshingly easy to read.

The microbes in our gut are in constant communication with our immune and nervous systems. We've discovered that having a lot of microbes is not enough, we need lots of different kinds of them; diversity is key. Eating a variety of different vegetables means that we're feeding a wide array of microbes – each microbe has its own favourite fibre. Other than the all-important fibre, fruit and vegetables also supply us with polyphenols - plant antioxidants - which also encourage the microbes' growth. Fermented vegetables such as sauerkraut and kimchi, and fermented soy such as tempeh, are some of their favourite foods.

Exercising, and especially exercising outdoors before eating – think walking – increases the numbers and the diversity of the microbes. We're going to be fasting between meals which allows these creatures to get on with their housekeeping jobs, such as repairing the lining of the gut and making vitamins. We're going to be reducing our stress levels by keeping regular hours – another habit they love. And we're going to be eating a diet of whole unprocessed protein and vegetables with no artificial additives and no emulsifiers – that's music to the microbe's ear.

Fast food destroys our old friends

What are the things they don't like? They don't like stress or lack of sleep and they're decimated by antibiotics. They don't like sugar or flying, or loud music. They hate fast food. Tim Spector, professor of genetic epidemiology at King's College, London is an expert on the microbiome (the collection of microbes in our gut, also known as the microbiota). Inspired by *'Supersize Me'* Morgan Spurlock's 2004 documentary (a month of junk food increased Spurlock's fat mass by 7%), Spector decided to run a similar study of his own. He was intrigued to discover what effects a fast food diet would have on the microbiome. You can read about it in Spector's book *The Diet Myth – the real science behind what we eat.*[3]

Spector's 22-year old son Tom happily took on the 10-day challenge for the one-man experiment. He alternated chicken nuggets with burgers. *'Although he had to keep his sugar levels high by having a regular Coke and a McFlurry ice-cream dessert (600 calories of sugar and saturated fat) with his main course, in the evening he could supplement the diet with vital extra nutrients supplied by crisps and beer'.*

But 6 days into the experiment Tom had had enough; he felt bloated and sluggish and by the 8th day he was getting sweats after he ate and he felt exhausted, but he kept to the deal he'd made with his dad and stuck it out. *"Before I started my father's fast food diet,"* Tom said, *"there were about 3,500 bacterial species in my gut, dominated by a type called firmicutes. Once on the diet I rapidly lost 1,300 species and my gut was dominated by a group called bacteroidetes. The implication is that the McDonald's diet killed 1,300 of my gut species".*

A tale of two diets

This area is a bit controversial but scientists generally agree that the healthiest diet and the one that works best to reduce inflammation is the Mediterranean diet (MD).[4] And Tom Spector's experimental fast-food diet is the antitheses of the MD and a good example of a pro-inflammatory diet. The MD diet includes lots of vegetables, some legumes (beans and chickpeas), fruit and nuts and some cereals. It's low in animal fat but includes lots of olive oil, and generally lots of fish too. It includes dairy products, mostly in the form of cheese or yoghurt, and moderate alcohol, mainly wine, with meals. The cereal bit is interesting because one study suggests that there are higher rates of celiac disease in Italy and that's possibly why it's so easy to find gluten-free spaghetti and pizza there.[5]

On the flipside of the MD is the pro-inflammatory diet (such as Spector's) which is high in refined carbs, sugars and trans-fats (think foods that are deep-fried in vegetable oils such as canola, rapeseed, sunflower etc.). And this kind of diet is, by its nature, also low in anti-inflammatory plant antioxidants and fibre from vegetables and nuts. And it's also too low in the anti-inflammatory oils from fish and olives.[6] A combination of a pro-inflammatory diet and a sedentary lifestyle is the recipe for a perfect storm of inflammation, immune system activation and friendly microbe destruction. When we sit down to eat we might ask ourselves not 'What would I like to eat' but 'What would *they* like to eat?'

1   Bloomfield, S. F. et al 2016. Time to abandon the hygiene hypothesis: new perspectives on allergic disease, the human microbiome, infectious disease prevention and the role of targeted hygiene. Perspectives in Public Health, 136(4):213-224. Available: http://journals.sagepub.com/doi/10.1177/1757913916650225 [Accessed 30 September 2018]

2   Knight, R. & Buhler, B. 2015. Follow Your Gut: The Enormous Impact of Tiny Microbes, New York, NY, Simon & Schuster: TED.

3   Spector, Tim. 2015. The Diet Myth: The real science behind what we eat, London, Weidenfeld & Nicolson

4   Sureda, A. et al 2018. Adherence to the Mediterranean Diet and Inflammatory Markers. Nutrients, 10(1):62. Available: https://www.mdpi.com/2072-6643/10/1/62/htm [Accessed 10 October 2018]

5   Volta, U. et al 2001. High prevalence of celiac disease in Italian general population. Digestive Diseases and Sciences, 46(7):1500-1505.

6   Giugliano, D., Ceriello, A. & Esposito, K. 2006. The Effects of Diet on Inflammation: Emphasis on the Metabolic Syndrome. Journal of the American College of Cardiology, 48(4):677-685. Available:https://www.sciencedirect.com/science/article/pii/S0735109706013350

•   Rook, G. A. W. The background to the Old Friend Hypothesis [Online]. Graham Rook. Available: http://www.grahamrook.net/OldFriends/oldfriends.html [Accessed 30 September 2018].

- Ozdal, T. et al 2016. The Reciprocal Interactions between Polyphenols and Gut Microbiota and Effects on Bioaccessibility. *Nutrients*, *8*(2):78. Available: https://www.mdpi.com/2072-6643/8/2/78 [Accessed 10 October 2018]

- Casas, R. & Estruch, R. 2016. Dietary Patterns, Foods, Nutrients and Chronic Inflammatory Disorders. Immunome Research, 12(2). Available: https://www.omicsonline.org/open-access/dietary-patterns-foods-nutrients-and-chronic-inflammatory-disorders-1745-7580-10000122.php?aid=78928 [Accessed 10 October 2018]

12: Resetting our Rhythm
- what makes us tick?

STRANGE THOUGH IT sounds we've got 'clock genes' which regulate the circadian rhythm in our bodies. They help to regulate, among other things, our sleep, body temperature and blood pressure. It's not just humans who have them, every organism on earth operates on a 24-hour clock. Our rhythm is vital to our health and disrupting it, getting out of sync, is associated with all kinds of illnesses, including psychiatric, metabolic and immune disorders, and even with addiction.[1]

A sure-fire way to disrupt our body clock is by looking at phones and iPads before we go to sleep. These devices emit blue light, daylight, and when we're looking at them at night, we prevent our pineal gland (a pea-sized organ in the centre of the brain) from producing melatonin.

If you look at the research into circadian rhythm, chronobiology, you might come across the word 'zeitgeber', which is German for 'time' and 'giver'.

A zeitgeber is a trigger which synchronises our human circadian rhythm, both to the earth's 24-hour light and dark cycle, and to the 12-month cycle of the year. In 2017, the Nobel Prize for Physiology or Medicine was awarded to Jeffrey Hall, Michael Robash and Michael Young for their discovery of how genes work together to control the circadian rhythm.[2] Other zeitgebers which help to get us back into a healthy rhythm include the time that we eat, the sort of food that we eat, how often we eat and when we exercise.

Melatonin – more than just a sleep hormone

Melatonin is our sleep hormone. When it begins to get dark in the evening, our temperature and our cortisol levels drop, and our melatonin levels rise, and that is the signal to sleep. That works well in Africa - the sun comes up at 6am, our cortisol levels increase, we wake up. The sun goes down at 6pm and we start winding down for the night as melatonin levels rise again. But that rhythm doesn't work so well in Northern hemisphere winters when it starts getting dark at 5pm and it isn't light again until 8am or so. We're not good at making melatonin unless it's dark and that means that TVs, phones and computers, inhibit its production.

But melatonin is not just a sleep hormone; it works as an antioxidant, and shows cancer protective properties[3,4] too. We know that we need all our hormones acting together as an orchestra, and melatonin is no exception. Women with hormone imbalance, including pre-menstrual syndrome/tension, or with an extreme version of this, premenstrual dysphoric disorder, suffer with circadian rhythm and sleep disturbance.[5] Research shows that when these women take melatonin supplements, and take steps to reset their rhythm, this can help to lessen the unpleasant symptoms.

But there's even more to it than that; melatonin is involved with our fat cells. Melatonin influences certain stem cells and pushes them towards bone cell, rather than fat cell production.[6] And it protects us against the growth of abnormally large fat cells, and abnormally large numbers of them. Without enough melatonin, our fat cells keep increasing in size, which pushes us ever further into a state of inflammation.

Burning fat while we sleep

I realise this sounds unlikely, but during the day, we're eating and we're in fat-storage mode. It's mainly overnight, when we're asleep, that our fat stores are broken down again. Under the influence of melatonin and the immune system, fat is burnt at night. We might think that our fat is just a pesky substance that can be hard to shift; in fact, the fat acts both as an endocrine (hormonal) and as an immune organ,[7,8] and it has wide-ranging effects on our metabolism. The release of all the signals and hormones our body produces is ruled by our circadian clocks. The immune system, when it's active and in repair mode overnight, breaks down fat, with the help of the liver, to fuel itself. And we wake up thinner – but only if we have enough melatonin.

Let's ensure we get enough melatonin by getting to bed earlier and avoiding bright lights and phones at night. It's possible to buy it over the counter and take it as a supplement in the US but we're not so lucky over here. Some of us, due to the lack of daylight in winter, suffer with the winter blues, SAD (seasonal affective disorder) and find that using light boxes during the day, and melatonin (2.5-3mg) at night, helps to restore our rhythm and our joie de vivre.

The time we go to bed, the time at which we exercise, and how often and when we eat, are some of the vital zeitgebers that are within our control. Eating breakfast is a zeitgeber; it tells our internal clock that it's the beginning of the day. When we eat in the way outlined in this book, eating 3 times a day with 5 hours between meals, and finishing dinner before 9pm, we are helping to reset our internal rhythm, and with that, we're naturally returning to health.

Grandma Pot was a strict timekeeper

Nutrition scientist Dr. Gerda Pot was intrigued both by her grandmother's good health, living healthily and independently into her

90s, and equally by her strict timekeeping when it came to meals. She wondered whether the two were connected and set out to find the answer: *'My research showed that people who had regular eating patterns had a lower risk of obesity though they consumed more calories'.*[9] And as the authors of a 2014 paper less pithily concluded: *'The consumption of beneficial food components, such as polyphenols, unsaturated fatty acids, and fiber, at suitable times would help to promote health in the same way as medication is administered at specific times in chronopharmacology. Not only the quality and quantity but also timing is important for nutrition'.*[10]

To recap: the programme that you are about to embark on includes 3 meals a day; there's a 5-hour gap between meals, and dinner must be finished by 9pm – it sounds as if it could be called the Grandma Pot diet. You naturally have more rhythm and routine in your life, your adrenals (the tiny organs sitting atop the kidneys that produce sex hormones, and the stress hormones, cortisol and adrenaline) will love you for it and so will your microbes.

1   Depoy, L. M., Mcclung, C. A. & Logan, R. W. 2017. Neural Mechanisms of Circadian Regulation of Natural and Drug Reward. Neural Plasticity, 2017, 1-14. Available: https://www.hindawi.com/journals/np/2017/5720842/ [Accessed 30 September 2018]

2   Hall, J. C., Rosbash, M. & Young, M. W. 2017. The 2017 Nobel Prize in Physiology or Medicine – Press release [Online]. Nobel Media AB. [Accessed 30 September 2018]. https://www.nobelprize.org/prizes/medicine/2017/press-release/

3   Asghari, M., Ghobadi, E., Moloudizargari, M., Fallah, M. and Abdollahi, M. (2018). Does the use of melatonin overcome drug resistance in cancer chemotherapy? Life Sciences, 196, 143-155.

4   Reiter, R., Rosales-Corral, S., Tan, D., Acuna-Castroviejo, D., Qin, L., Yang, S. and Xu, K. (2017). Melatonin, a Full Service Anti-Cancer Agent: Inhibition of Initiation, Progression and Metastasis. International Journal of Molecular Sciences, 18(4):843. Available: https://www.mdpi.com/1422-0067/18/4/843/htm [Accessed 10 October 2018].

5   Shechter, A. & Boivin, D. B. 2010. Sleep, Hormones, and Circadian Rhythms throughout the Menstrual Cycle in Healthy Women and Women with Premenstrual Dysphoric Disorder. International Journal of Endocrinology, 2010, 259345. Available: https://www.hindawi.com/journals/ije/2010/259345/ [Accessed 30 September 2018].

6   Basoli, V., Santaniello, S., Cruciani, S., Ginesu, G., Cossu, M., Delitala, A., Serra, P., Ventura, C. and Maioli, M. (2017). Melatonin and Vitamin D Interfere with the Adipogenic Fate of Adipose-Derived Stem Cells. International Journal of Molecular Sciences, 18(5):981. Available: https://www.mdpi.com/1422-0067/18/5/981/htm [Accessed 10 October 2018].

7   Grant, R. and Dixit, V. (2015). Adipose tissue as an immunological organ. Obesity, 23(3):512-518. Available: https://onlinelibrary.wiley.com/doi/full/10.1002/oby.21003 [Accessed 10 October 2018]

8   Coelho, M., Oliveira, T. and Fernandes, R. (2013). State of the art paper Biochemistry of adipose tissue: an endocrine organ. *Archives of Medical Science*, 9(2):191-200. Available: https://www.termedia.pl/State-of-the-art-paper-Biochemistry-of-adipose-tissue-an-endocrine-organ,19,20246,1,1.html [Accessed 10 October 2018].

9   Pot, G. K., Almoosawi, S. & Stephen, A. M. 2016. Meal irregularity and cardiometabolic consequences: results from observational and intervention studies. Proceedings of the Nutrition Society, 75(04):475-486.

10   Oike, H., Oishi, K. & Kobori, M. 2014. Nutrients, Clock Genes, and Chrononutrition. Current Nutrition Reports, 3(3):204-212. Available: https://link.springer.com/article/10.1007%2Fs13668-014-0082-6 [Accessed 30 September 2018].

•   Pantazopoulos, H., Gamble, K., Stork, O. & Amir, S. 2018. Circadian Rhythms in Regulation of Brain Processes and Role in Psychiatric Disorders. Neural Plasticity, 2018, 1-3. Available:https://www.hindawi.com/journals/np/2018/5892657/ [Accessed 30 September 2018].

•   Wolverton, M. 2013. Living by the clock: The science of chronobiology [Online]. Medical Xpress. Available: https://medicalxpress.com/news/2013-06-clock-science-chronobiology.html [Accessed 30 September 2018].

•   De Lange, C. 2016. In Sync: How to take control of your many body clocks [Online]. New Scientist. Available: https://www.newscientist.com/article/mg23030690-300-in-sync-how-to-take-control-of-your-many-body-clocks/ [Accessed 30 September 2018].

•   Pagano, E., Spinedi, E. and Gagliardino, J. (2016). White Adipose Tissue and Circadian Rhythm Dysfunctions in Obesity: Pathogenesis and Available Therapies. Neuroendocrinology, 104(4):347-363. Available: https://www.karger.com/Article/FullText/453317 [Accessed 30 September 2018].

•   Kooijman, S., et al (2015). Prolonged daily light exposure increases body fat mass through attenuation of brown adipose tissue activity. Proceedings of the National Academy of Sciences, 112(21), pp.6748-6753. Available: http://www.pnas.org/content/112/21/6748 [Accessed 30 September 2018].

13: Sunshine and Vitamin D

I **GREW UP** in the era of sun worship – we'd baste ourselves with Mazola or Baby Oil and spend our summers roasting in the sun and the browner we got the better we felt. On our childhood beach holidays it was low protection Ambre Solaire, probably with SPF of 6 or so, or nothing. But now we're terrified of the sun and it makes me sad, and slightly concerned, to see children on summer beaches wrapped up in Lycra suits topped with sunhats, their faces slathered in factor 50 sun screen.

Total protection from the sun is the path to certain vitamin D deficiency, including a resurgence of rickets, not to mention pain disorders, depression and osteoporosis. We can't make vitamin D if we're putting factor 8 or higher on our skin. I don't use any sun protection, even on holiday. Between about 11am-2pm I sit in the shade, I don't do mad dogs and Englishmen. Without sunshine and the effects of vitamin D we humans would not be here at all.

Picture this. In the old days we'd be hunting and gathering through the summer (or working the land, a bit later on in our history). We'd be outside all day, not wearing too many clothes, and the cholesterol in our skin would be making vitamin D. Food was relatively plentiful and after the long lean months of winter we'd be eating as much as we could and putting on a little fat. The vitamin D was stored in our fat.

As the summer drew to an end and autumn set in, we, like the hedgehog, ate more fruit and eating the fruit made us hungry for more and we accumulated a little more fat. Of course we didn't have the luxury of hibernation and had to carry on searching for food over the winter months. And the little fat we'd accumulated over the joyful summer would break down and, as the fat broke down, vitamin D was released with it and helped us stave off infections over the winter. But now we get as thin as we can before the summer and once in the sun we cover ourselves in high SPF creams and lotions so it's hardly surprising that as a nation we are almost all vitamin D deficient.

Sunshine melts our fat

We not only get more sleep and feel happier and less stressed on holiday but we also get more light and that might explain why, despite eating more food and exercising less, we often lose weight on a summer holiday. One study could help to explain why: Researchers at the University of Alberta[1] found out that the fat cells which lie just below our skin shrink when they're exposed to the blue light from the sun. The sunshine is melting our fat! This was a breakthrough study by scientists who've found another reason, aside from improving our vitamin D levels, to bask in the sunshine. 'It's early days' they write, 'but it's not a giant leap to suppose that the light that regulates our circadian rhythm, received through our eyes, may also have the same impact through the fat cells near our skin.'

Our incredible immune system, which is designed to protect us from wounds and bacterial and viral infections, has been chronically activated by our diet and lifestyle. We have the power to overturn this inflammation and head back towards great health and vitality, and that power is literally in our hands and feet. We can pick up our knife and fork and eat the foods that support our health and we can choose to get off the sofa or the office chair and take to our feet and walk. With the *Human Being Diet* we are going to eat natural food, get the rhythm back into our lives, sleep better, feel more energetic and quell the low-grade inflammation. We'll *feel* the benefits on the inside and *see* them on the outside.

1   Ondrusova, K. et al. 2017. Subcutaneous white adipocytes express a light sensitive signaling pathway mediated via a melanopsin/TRPC channel axis. Scientific Reports, 7:16332. Available: https://www.nature.com/articles/s41598-017-16689-4 [Accessed 30 September 2018].

•   Wierzbicka, J., Piotrowska, A. & Zmijewski, M. A. 2014. The renaissance of vitamin D. Acta Biochimica Polonica, 61(4):679-686. Available: http://www.actabp.pl/pdf/4_2014/679.pdf [Accessed 30 September 2018].

PART 2: The Solution

The 4 Phases and the 10 Rules

1. Phase 1 – Prep: 2 days - lots of vegetables
2. Phase 2 – Reset: 14 days –super strict; weighing all food, no oil/grains/sugar/alcohol
3. Phase 3 – Burn: 10 weeks – or until goal weight is reached. Oil is reintroduced; weekly treat meal
4. Phase 4 – Forever

And here are the 10 rules:

1. Eat 3 meals a day and fast for 5 hours between meals – no tea or coffee between meals, just water
2. Begin each meal with a couple of bites of protein and have one type of protein per meal
3. Don't eat for longer than one hour (except at weekly treat meals)
4. Finish eating by 9pm
5. Drink the right amount of water (about 35ml per kilo of body weight)
6. Eat an apple a day with breakfast, lunch or dinner
7. No oil and no alcohol for the first 16 days
8. No wheat and no grains for the first 16 days
9. No cardio exercise for the first 16 days
10. No sugar (and no honey or fake sugar)

In this chapter we'll discuss the 10 rules in detail and the reasoning behind them because once you understand why they're important you'll find it easier to follow them. And then we'll discuss the 4 phases of the programme.

Rule 1: Eat 3 meals a day and fast for at least 5 hours between each meal

THIS IS THE end of eating little and often and is probably the most important rule of all. Two of the many hormones involved in weight loss/weight gain are insulin and glucagon and they're a bit like Jekyll and Hyde – they never appear together. Insulin is the fat-storage hormone and glucagon is the fat-burner. When we're fasting between meals we have lower insulin and higher glucagon. And when we sit down to eat we should feel relaxed, that way our digestion and absorption works better.

Brick factories close their doors

Imagine our cells are like brick factories – we need truck drivers to deliver the sand to the factory to make the bricks. But if too much sand keeps arriving at the factory and the factory runs out of storage space it has to close its doors. The sand gets dumped outside. It's just like that with sugar in the blood – the cell has receptors, like doors, on its surface and once a cell is packed with sugar it closes the doors and won't let any more in. This is insulin resistance – insulin is the truck driver that delivers the sand. The foreman in charge of the factory rings the owners and he gets the go-ahead to make storage depots outside the factory. The storage depots are our fat cells.

But when blood sugar levels get too low – when we haven't eaten anything for a few hours (this is the factory running low on the sand it needs to make the bricks) a hormone called glucagon is released and we begin to break down our fat stores to give us energy. Glucagon is the foreman yelling 'we need more sand and we need it NOW! Get back to work you lot!' After about 4 hours of fasting, depending on what we ate at our last meal, we can start to burn fat. This is because the insulin is low enough for the body to release glucagon, the fat-burner. As long as we finish eating before 9pm (8pm would be even better) our insulin levels will be at their lowest overnight; that's why we're in fat-burning mode while we sleep.

Eating 3 meals a day with nothing between meals except water, and having 5 hours between each meal, not only gives the digestive system a rest, it also helps to reset and re-establish our circadian rhythm.

Sabotaging fat burning

No coffee or tea between meals. After a meal of protein and vegetables, our insulin and sugar increase gently to reach a peak before they start to recede again. Although black coffee or tea doesn't contain any calories it does contain caffeine. And caffeine affects the nervous system and puts us into mild fight or flight; sugar is released into the blood stream from storage sites and fat burning stops. It's because of the effect caffeine can have on blood sugar that some diabetes experts forbid their patients to drink coffee, even decaf coffee.[1] But for most healthy people it seems that a cup of black tea or coffee with or just after eating, has a minimal effect on blood sugar and doesn't interfere with fat burning.

We know that fight or flight is our ancient response to any kind of stress and that it triggers a cascade of hormonal activity, including the release of adrenaline and cortisol. Blood sugar increases, glucagon decreases and fat burning stops. It's as simple as that. We don't want to interfere with the decreasing sugar and insulin or we don't get to the fat burning part – that's why it's so important to stick to water only between meals.

Any time you snack, or drink anything other than water between meals, you're sabotaging your body's attempt to burn fat. Tea or coffee with milk (milk contains sugar called lactose) acts like a mini-meal which means there's a small rise in blood sugar and fat burning stops. And as we've learned, even black tea, green tea, or black coffee (decaf or not) can stop us burning fat.

If you're a snacker you've inadvertently trained your brain and body to expect food every 2-3 hours or so. Your insulin never gets low enough for glucagon to appear. It's going to take a few days to stabilise your blood sugar again. While you're making your new habit of fasting between meals you'll probably feel hungry and angry – hangry. But stick with it, keep the faith, your body will adapt and pretty soon you will be making the vital change from carb burner to fat burner.

The fat-burning feeling

Reframe any negative nagging feeling of hunger into a positive feeling of, 'I love this feeling, I'm burning fat, this is what it feels like!' It's normal to feel hungry when you start. Sticking to the 5-hour rule and combining the right amount of protein and vegetables means very soon you won't feel hungry between meals at all because your blood sugar will be stable and your insulin levels will be lower. By getting rid of the snacks you're reminding your body to reconnect with all its old tricks of raising blood sugar levels again.

Another benefit of fasting between meals, rather than grazing or snacking, is the effect it has on our digestive health. When we fast between meals a sort of sweeping action, which starts in the stomach and travels down through the intestines, takes place and this is thought to serve as a housekeeping role. Undigested food and fibres and bacteria are swept through the digestive system in a cleansing sweep which occurs every 1.5 to 2 hours, but it only happens when we're fasting; this sweep is catchily called the migrating motor complex.[2]

To summarise, fasting between meals is beneficial because:

- Insulin levels are lower, which means we can burn fat for energy
- It allows the microbes to get on with their housekeeping jobs
- It gives the digestive system, including the pancreas, a rest
- It lowers inflammation
- It stimulates the detoxing sweep of the intestinal tract

1   Greenberg, J. A., Owen, D. R. & Geliebter, A. 2009. Decaffeinated Coffee and Glucose Metabolism in Young Men. Diabetes Care, 33, 278-280. Available: http://care.diabetesjournals.org/content/33/2/278 [Accessed 30 September 2018].

2   Deloose, E. & Tack, J. 2015. Redefining the functional roles of the gastrointestinal migrating motor complex and motilin in small bacterial overgrowth and hunger signaling. American Journal of Physiology - Gastrointestinal and Liver Physiology, 310(4):G228-G233. Available: https://www.physiology.org/doi/full/10.1152/ajpgi.00212.2015 [Accessed 30 September 2018].

Rule 2: Begin each meal with protein and eat one type of protein per meal

WHEN WE START to eat, a message is sent to the pancreas as well as the brain. The pancreas is where insulin and our digestive enzymes are produced. The pancreas releases digestive enzymes into the small intestine, but it doesn't wait for the food to reach the gut before it gets to work. The food being chewed in our mouth sends information to the pancreas about which enzymes it needs to produce so by the time the food gets to the gut the enzymes are ready too.

If we've been used to eating lots of carbohydrates, including sugar, fruit and grains, the pancreas gets trigger-happy and with the first sign of a carbohydrate coming in it ramps up insulin production. High blood sugar is viewed as a danger signal; the pancreas doesn't wait before going into overdrive to make sure there's enough insulin to get the sugar out of harm's way. And we know that all that insulin is not going to make us thinner because it's a very efficient fat-storage hormone.

Messaging the pancreas

Some of the enzymes produced by the pancreas include amylase for sugar and carbohydrate digestion, lipase to digest fats, and proteases for protein digestion. So far so good. But, as mentioned, carbohydrates in the mouth (even good carbs like vegetables) send another message to the pancreas – they pass on the message to release insulin. If we start a meal with some protein, a couple of bites of egg, meat, chicken or fish, or some nuts or seeds, and *then* have the carbohydrate, the pancreas produces less insulin and that's a good thing.

The 3 food groups

- *Carbohydrates – A carbohydrate is a food that is converted by our bodies into sugar. Fruit and fruit juice, vegetables, legumes, grains (including pseudo-grains like quinoa and buckwheat) honey, all syrups and sugar are carbohydrates. And all carbohydrates stimulate insulin release. The more fibre these foods contain the longer they take to digest and the less impact they have on raising our blood sugar and insulin levels. But ultimately they all get converted into sugar.*
  Vegetables and pulses, which contain fibre, count as 'good' carbs. We used to think that vegetables were 'free' in terms of calories but now we know that because they are carbohydrates and carbohydrates break down into sugar, if we want to lose weight, we must limit the amount of vegetables we eat.
  Refined carbohydrates, including bread, rice, biscuits and cakes as well as fruit juice and many breakfast cereals, essentially have the fibre stripped out which means they hit the bloodstream as sugar much faster and result in higher insulin levels and more hunger.
  Odd as it might seem, we do not need carbohydrates to stay alive but we can't do without fats and proteins.

- *Proteins – Eggs, fish and shellfish, poultry, red meat, nuts and seeds are protein foods. Pulses like beans, chickpeas and lentils, count as proteins in vegan/vegetarian diets but mostly, other than soy, they contain as much carbohydrate as protein. Yoghurt, cheese, milk and soy products including tofu are also classed as protein foods. Most cheese is a combination of protein and fat but it's generally lower in carbohydrate than milk or yoghurt because the friendly bacteria it contains have converted the sugars into lactic acid. Although quinoa is often billed as a good protein it actually contains roughly five times more carbohydrate than protein. Getting enough protein is vital for weight loss. All foods, with the exception of oils, contain some protein.*

- *Fats – The essential fats, the ones we must include in our diet, are the omega 3 and omega 6 family of fats. We get these fats from fish and animals and from nuts and seeds including walnuts, flaxseed and sunflower seeds. These are the fats that are vital for our overall health, for our brain and eyes, and for our immune system and hormones. Fat contains twice as many calories as carbohydrate but it keeps us going for longer without feeling hungry.*

Pearl necklaces

Proteins are made from long chains of individual amino acids – a bit like pearl necklaces. The proteins are broken down into single amino acids in the gut. They travel from the gut to the liver and that's where they are rearranged into the proteins that we need. The proteins that make our muscles, our skin, our hair, and all our hormones and immune cells, are made from the protein that we eat. So that expression 'You are what you eat' really is true. It's a bizarre thought that our biceps are literally made from the fish, chicken and eggs that we've eaten.

Of the 20 amino acids that make up proteins, 9 are termed 'essential'. Essential means we can't make those amino acids in our bodies, they must be included in our diet; all the proteins that we need can be produced from these 9 amino acids. Scientists have long debated about how best to measure protein quality. The US FDA and the Food & Agriculture Organization of the WHO adopted a new way to best measure it: *Protein Digestibility-Corrected Amino Acid Score* (PDCAAS).[1] PDCAAS is the standard for evaluating protein quality because it's a measure not only of the amino acids a food contains, but also of our ability to digest them.

Combining 2 or more different proteins within a meal can have 2 different effects. The best scenario is that we get a good balance of amino acids to make the proteins our bodies need. But what may happen is that we get the balance wrong, which means some of the protein we eat gets wasted; that protein gets converted into ammonia which is excreted via our kidneys.

Perfect proteins

Clued up vegetarians know that they need to combine different plant foods to optimise the amount of protein that they absorb. Combining rice with beans for example, rather than having rice *or* beans, makes for a well-balanced protein meal. A complete protein food is one that contains all 9 essential amino acids. All these complete protein foods, with the exception of soy, are animal derived: casein (milk protein), eggs, milk (which contains casein and whey), whey protein and chicken are the highest quality proteins in our diet. Soy, which is very nearly as complete a protein as beef, also ranks high on the list of the best quality proteins. Plant proteins, as found in vegetables, grains, nuts and seeds, lack one or more of the essential amino acids, which is why they must be combined to give vegetarians and vegans the protein that they need.

Sticking to one type of animal protein per meal means that more protein is used and absorbed with little waste and less work for the kidneys. To recap, combining animal protein with plant protein, or combining different types of animal protein (as in surf & turf) means less protein absorption, whereas combining different types of plant proteins (as in rice and beans) means protein absorption is optimal.

To summarise, beginning each meal with protein and eating one type of protein per meal is beneficial because:

- Less insulin is produced
- More protein is absorbed
- We put less pressure on our kidneys

1   Schaafsma, G. 2000. The Protein Digestibility–Corrected Amino Acid Score. The Journal of Nutrition, 130(7) 1865S-1867S. Available: https://academic.oup.com/jn/article/130/7/1865S/4686203 [Accessed 30 September 2018]

•   Monirujjaman, M. & Ferdouse, A. 2014. Metabolic and Physiological Roles of Branched-Chain Amino Acids. Advances in Molecular Biology, 2014, 1-6. Available: https://www.hindawi.com/journals/amb/2014/364976/ [Accessed 30 September 2018]

•   Higdon, J., Drake, V. J., Angelo, G. & Jump, D. B. 2014. Essential Fatty Acids [Online]. Linus Pauling Institute. Available: https://lpi.oregonstate.edu/mic/other-nutrients/essential-fatty-acids [Accessed 30 September 2018].

Rule 3: Don't eat for longer than one hour

IF WE'RE EATING 3 meals a day and we need a 5 hour fast between meals and we must finish eating by 9pm, we'd better ensure that we eat our meals in a timely fashion, but let's not eat too quickly – that can make us fatter too.[1] We know that when we eat a meal, our insulin and blood sugar increases – this is normal. This is the body saying 'good, food's coming in to give us energy and feed our muscles, and if there's enough of it we can store some of this food as fat for the next time we don't have anything coming in'. And this is why you can have black tea or coffee with food – blood sugar is going up anyway as a result of eating and it's not going to spike because the food blunts caffeine's effect.

The 'don't eat for longer than an hour' rule means we can't slip back into our old ways of grazing – we eat our meal, have black tea or coffee if we want it and, once the food has been processed, fat burning commences. If we keep on eating, our insulin keeps on increasing which means that we are in fat-storage, rather that fat-burning, mode.

Keep the window open

To recap: we're eating 3 times a day, we finish eating by 9pm and we fast for 5 hours between meals. Eating in this way not only gives us more fat-burning time, it also pushes us into a rhythm and routine which has wide ranging positive effects on us. One of the positive effects is that it stabilises our blood sugar, and lowers our insulin, which means we are less hungry between meals. Remember that the

5-hour fast between meals begins when we finish the meal (not when we start it). Understanding that just a little snack, or a cup of coffee, or herb tea, will completely sabotage that 5-hour fat burning window, and the hormonal reset, makes it easier to avoid temptation.

To summarise, not eating for longer than 1 hour at mealtimes is beneficial because:

- It helps to push us into a rhythm and routine that's good for us
- It prevents us from grazing and allows insulin to decrease between meals
- It gives us more fat-burning time

1   Hurst, Y. & Fukuda, H. 2018. Effects of changes in eating speed on obesity in patients with diabetes: a secondary analysis of longitudinal health check-up data. BMJ Open,8(1) pe019589. Available: https://bmjopen.bmj.com/content/bmjopen/8/1/e019589.full.pdf [Accessed 10 October 2018].

Rule 4: Finish eating by 9pm

WHEN WE FINISH eating and digesting in the evening, our insulin levels begin to drop and should be at their lowest overnight. The lower our insulin level is before bed, the more fat-burning we can do. Eating and drinking late into the night means our insulin is still high, and as a result we're in fat-storage mode, rather than fat-burning mode. Some of us used to scoff at our cousins across the Atlantic for eating dinner at 6 or 7, but they were right – a gap of at least 3 hours between eating and sleeping is perfect and maximises our fat-burning potential.

 Night time is fat burning time. We burn more fat when we are asleep than when we're awake. How is that possible? One of the reasons is that our immune system is active overnight and breaking down fat to fuel itself. it's prowling around looking for bugs that might have sneaked in during the day. And at the same time, overnight, the body is in repair mode; repairing tissues is another of the immune system's jobs. That terrible aching that we experience with flu is partly because the immune system has been focusing on killing bacteria or viruses and hasn't had a chance to switch into repair mode.

And the other reason, as we've learned, is because insulin is at its lowest overnight. This is why we are literally thinner in the morning. But if we're still digesting and absorbing food that we've eaten too late, or too much of, and if we don't get enough sleep, we don't get the fat-burning time. When we sleep for 6 hours of less, the result is lower leptin and increased ghrelin levels —a bad combination of hormones that increases hunger.[1, 2, 3]

To summarise, it is important to finish eating by 9pm because:

- Sleeping time is fat-burning time but only if our insulin is low overnight
- Lower insulin and sugar overnight means less inflammation

1   Wang X., Sparks J., K., Shawn D Youngstedt S. 2018. Influence of sleep restriction on weight loss outcomes associated with caloric restriction, Sleep 41(5) zsy027.

2   Rynders, C., Bergouignan A., Kealey E., Daniel H. Bessesen D. 2017. Ability to adjust nocturnal fat oxidation in response to overfeeding predicts 5-year weight gain in adults. Obesity (Silver Spring) 25(5):873-880. Available: https://onlinelibrary. wiley.com/doi/full/10.1002/oby.21807 [Accessed 30 September 2018].

3   Magkos, F., Smith, G. I., Reeds, D. N., Okunade, A., Patterson, B. W. & Mittendorfer, B. 2014. One day of overfeeding impairs nocturnal glucose but not fatty acid homeostasis in overweight men. Obesity (Silver Spring), 22(2):435-440. Available: https://onlinelibrary.wiley.com/doi/pdf/10.1002/oby.20562 [Accessed 30 September 2018].

Rule 5: Drink the right amount of water

THE ADVICE IS to drink 35ml of water per kilo of body weight – so someone of 60kg would need just over two litres a day and someone weighing 100 kg or more would need 3.5-4 litres. It's a good idea to add electrolyte drops (sodium, potassium and magnesium) to your water. Electrolytes not only make the water taste better but they also improve our hydration. Water is vitally important; it's like the spark plug in the machine which transmits energy round the body.

Dehydration is another danger signal (like stress, or high insulin or blood sugar) and this one tells the body to conserve energy – lack of water is perceived as a much more serious problem than lack of food. Theoretically, when we're dehydrated, the metabolic rate drops and we burn fewer calories. Sometimes people are concerned about drinking too much, but unless you're out clubbing, it's difficult to drink too much water. Our problem is much more likely to be under-drinking than over-drinking. A good gauge of hydration is the colour of your urine – ideally it would be lightly coloured, more like Pinot Grigio than straw.

Ghrelin the hunger gremlin

When our stomach is empty, i.e. when there's no food inside it, it shrinks, and as it shrinks our hunger hormone, ghrelin, is released by the stomach itself. And ghrelin says to the brain 'there's nothing here, you'd better eat something'. But if you drink a big glass of water, ½ a litre or so, you stretch out your stomach and ghrelin slinks away. Before I saw the rat research[1] that suggests sparkling/fizzy water increases ghrelin, I used to say that fizzy water is certainly better than no water, but now I'm not so sure – for best results drink it flat.

Have a look at Peta Bee's article for *The Times* in March 2016, she wrote about the effect of water on weight loss: '*Here's the Water Diet (yes really)*'. She reports that Ruopeng An, researching at the University of Illinois, found that the people who drank 1-3 extra glasses of water a day were less drawn to sugar and salt and that they consumed fewer calories.[2] And in another study researchers studying obese adults found that the ones who drank ½ litre of water thirty minutes before each meal lost 3 pounds more than the ones who didn't – in fact they lost about 4.5kg over the course of the 12-week study.[3]

The best way to drink water is not to sip it through the day but to drink it caveman style, half a litre (a pint) in one go. Drink the first ½ litre as soon as you get out of bed in the morning – that's the most important time to rehydrate. And drink at least another 1.5 litres before lunch. Make drinking more water your greatest new habit. As discussed in Peta Bee's article, medics have long scoffed at the idea that drinking lots of water is beneficial in any way, for weight loss or anything else. But clinically I have seen again and again that the people who drink enough water, and who drink it early in the day, get the speediest weight loss results. And it's good for our skin - think 'plum' not 'prune'. And it's a great energiser too.

To summarise, it's important that we drink enough water, because water helps us:

- To keeps ghrelin, the hunger hormone away
- Speed up weight loss
- Stay alert and energised

1   Eweis, D. S., Abed, F. & Stiban, J. 2017. Carbon dioxide in carbonated beverages induces ghrelin release and increased food consumption in male rats: Implications on the onset of obesity. Obesity Research & Clinical Practice, 11(5):534-543. Available: https://www.stat.tamu.edu/~suhasini/CO2beverage.pdf [Accessed 30 September 2018].

2   An, R. & Mccaffrey, J. 2016. Plain water consumption in relation to energy intake and diet quality among US adults, 2005-2012. Journal of Human Nutrition and Dietetics, 29(5)624-632.

3   Parretti, H. M.et al 2015. Efficacy of water preloading before main meals as a strategy for weight loss in primary care patients with obesity: RCT. Obesity (Silver Spring), 23(9):1785-1791. Available: https://onlinelibrary.wiley.com/doi/full/10.1002/oby.21167 [Accessed 30 September 2018].

Rule 6: Eat an apple a day

AN APPLE A day is the only compulsory fruit on the programme – and although official advice is currently to eat five servings of fruit and vegetables a day, we'd be better off eating much more in the way of vegetables than fruit. A tongue in cheek paper appeared in the British Medical Journal in November 2013. The study's authors set out to discover the effects on the over 50s of being prescribed either an apple or a statin a day. They concluded that *'a one hundred and fifty year old health promotion message is able to match modern medicine and is likely to have fewer side effects'* and *'an apple a day or a statin is equally likely to keep the doctor at bay'*.[1] They taste good too.

According to Caroline Taggart, author of *An Apple a Day: Old fashioned proverbs and why they still work (2011)* the original proverb was not 'an apple a day keeps the doctor away' but: 'eat an apple on going to bed, and you'll keep the doctor from earning his bread'. But we won't be having our apple at bedtime, we'll be having it with breakfast, lunch or dinner.

Apple pectin magic

Apples contain a special kind of fibre called pectin and studies have shown all sorts of pectin health benefits from reducing cholesterol to reducing radiation levels in children in Chernobyl.[2] It's also been shown to reduce colon cancer (in rats) and to inhibit bacteria such as staphylococcus.[3] Pectin binds with toxins in the gut and helps to increase the volume of the stool, thus promoting regularity (i.e. it can act as a laxative). It also helps us to feel fuller. Apples are a good source of plant antioxidants called polyphenols.[4] Diets rich in polyphenols have been found to protect against the development and progression of several chronic conditions including cancer, diabetes, cardiovascular problems, and they have anti-aging effects too.[5,6] The combination of polyphenols and pectin is beloved by our microbes and encourages their growth.

Some people have a condition known as oral allergy syndrome (OAS)[7] and when they eat apples (and other fruit including plums, peaches, pears, and raw nuts) they suffer with itchy mouth, ears and throat and may also get swollen lips or facial hives. There is a crossover between OAS and hayfever; people who suffer from hayfever are more likely to experience OAS. If eating apples gives you these symptoms try eating them in a different way. Peeling the apple can help, as can putting it in a blender, or baking it in the oven, or even grating it.

Apple cider vinegar for cravings

Apple cider vinegar (ACV) has been used by generations of women to help them lose weight, despite the lack of scientific evidence until 2017/2018.[8,9] There are several rat and mouse studies that suggest it helps to reduce cravings and can even improve cholesterol levels. But at last, in 2017 a meta-analysis (a review of all the published studies) appeared that did show some benefits of ACV in humans: '*Results suggest that consuming vinegar (about 1 - 2 tablespoons) with a meal can reduce postprandial glucose and insulin responses in both healthy participants and those with insulin resistance or diabetes.*'[8]

In clinical practice people commonly report that it helps to reduce sugar cravings and they feel less bloated after eating. Apple cider vinegar contains malic acid and it is the malic acid that has both anti-bacterial and anti-fungal properties. So eat an apple with a meal every day, and add apple cider vinegar to salads or add 1-2 tablespoons to warm water and sip it with your meal. If you're wondering if you can substitute apple juice, even if it's fresh, for an apple, the answer is no! If you juice your apple you're missing out on the wonderful fibre that it contains.

To summarise, an apple a day is important because it:

- Contains pectin fibre which helps us detoxify
- Contains plant antioxidants, polyphenols, which protect us against diseases
- Feeds the good gut microbes
- Just might keep the doctor away

1   Briggs, A. D. M., Mizdrak, A. & Scarborough, P. 2013. A statin a day keeps the doctor away: comparative proverb assessment modelling study. BMJ: British Medical Journal, 347(dec17 2), pp.f7267-f7267.
    Available: https://www.bmj.com/content/347/bmj.f7267 [Accessed 30 September 2018].

2   Nesterenko, V. B., Nesterenko, A. V., Babenko, V. I., Yerkovich, T. V. & Babenko, I. V. 2004. Reducing the 137Cs-load in the organism of "Chernobyl" children with apple-pectin. Swiss Medical Weekly, 134(1-2):24-27.

3   Martinov, J et al. 2017. Apple pectin-derived oligosaccharides produce carbon dioxide radical anion in Fenton reaction and prevent growth of Escherichia coli and Staphylococcus aureus. Food Research International,100, 132-136

4   Lima G., Vianello F., Corrêa C., da Silva Campos R., Borguini M. 2014. Polyphenols in Fruits and Vegetables and Its Effect on Human Health. Food and Nutrition Sciences, 5(11):1065-1082. Available: http://file.scirp.org/Html/11-2701121_46941.htm [Accessed 10 October 2018]

5   Koutsos, A., Tuohy, K. M. & Lovegrove, J. A. 2015. Apples and Cardiovascular Health—Is the Gut Microbiota a Core Consideration? Nutrients, 7(6):3959-3998. Available: https://www.mdpi.com/2072-6643/7/6/3959/htm [Accessed 30 September 2018].

6   Cory, H., Passarelli, S., Szeto, J., Tamez, M., Mattei, J. 2018. The Role of Polyphenols in Human Health and Food Systems: A Mini-Review. Frontiers in Nutrition, 5, 87. Available: https://www.frontiersin.org/articles/10.3389/fnut.2018.00087/full [Accessed 30 September 2018].

7   The Anaphylaxis Campaign. 2015. Oral Allergy Syndrome [Online]. The Anaphylaxis Campaign. Available: https://www.anaphylaxis.org.uk/wp-content/uploads/2015/06/Oral-allergy-version-8-formatted-with-AC-logo-and-name-updated.pdf [Accessed 30 September 2018].

8   Shishehbor, F., Mansoori, A. & Shirani, F. 2017. Vinegar consumption can attenuate postprandial glucose and insulin responses; a systematic review and meta-analysis of clinical trials. Diabetes Research and Clinical Practice, 127, 1-9.

9   Siddiqui, F. J., Assam, P. N., De Souza, N. N., Sultana, R., Dalan, R. & Chan, E.
     S.-Y. 2018. Diabetes Control: Is Vinegar a Promising Candidate to Help Achieve
     Targets? Journal of Evidence-based Integrative Medicine, 23, 2156587217753004.
     Available: http://journals.sagepub.com/doi/full/10.1177/2156587217753004
     [Accessed 30 September 2018]

Rule 7: No oil and no alcohol for 16 days

THE NO OIL and no alcohol rule is essentially designed to give the liver a holiday. Our liver is an extraordinary organ – it might look like a giant slug but its healthy function is critically important to our health. The liver weighs in at a hefty 3 pounds, which is roughly the same as the brain and curiously about the same weight as our gut flora – the healthy bacteria which live in the gut.

Some of the jobs the liver is responsible for include fat burning, balancing blood sugar, making and breaking down proteins and hormones, neutralising toxins in the blood, including alcohol and drugs like paracetamol, and vitamin storage. In fact it has to detoxify everything from cigarette smoke to exhaust fumes to the chemical products we put on our skin. And we need our liver for fat digestion too, because it makes bile which is stored in the gall bladder. Bile is released when we eat fats and oils and it acts in a similar way to dishwashing liquid to break up, or emulsify, the fats in our diet so that we can digest and absorb them along with the fat-soluble vitamins, A, D, E and K.

It's a liver holiday

Problems with the liver can occur, including 'Fatty liver'. This is when the liver becomes sluggish because it's accumulated too much fat, and it no longer performs its tasks with any enthusiasm. Fatty liver could be the consequence of eating too much sugar and too many carbohydrates and/or drinking too much alcohol or even eating too much fruit.

Fructose, fruit sugar, is okay in small amounts (an apple a day). But too much fruit can result in non-alcoholic fatty liver disease (NAFLD) and supermarket fruit juice really should carry a health warning. Fructose encourages the liver to make fat and it's pro-inflammatory[1] and it makes us hungry too. For overall health and for the liver's sake in particular, keep it to a minimum. Fatty liver symptoms can include difficulty losing weight, irritability, itchy skin, nausea, heat intolerance, and PMT/PMS or heavy periods.

So to encourage the liver to get on with the fat burning, a 2 week liver holiday is in order. It's oil and alcohol-free, and, with the addition of light, nutritious meals and green vegetables you will have your liver fawning with gratitude. And during this time, you can still eat nutritious fatty foods including oily fish such as salmon, and avocado, nuts and seeds but no added fat or oil is to be used.

To summarise, the rule of no oil and no alcohol for 16 days is in place to:

- Give the liver a rest
- Allow the liver to get on with detoxification and fat burning

---

1   Jegatheesan, P. and De Bandt, J. 2017.
     Fructose and NAFLD: The Multifaceted Aspects of Fructose Metabolism. *Nutrients*, 9(3), p.230. Available: https://www.mdpi.com/2072-6643/9/3/230/htm [Accessed 10 October 2018]

Rule 8: No wheat and no grains for 16 days

DON'T MEAN to sound dramatic but I do sometimes think, if everyone was to stop eating wheat I wouldn't have much to do. Wheat makes us hungry and bloated and messes with our brain chemistry. And it makes the gut leaky which activates the immune system. Even if you don't think it's causing you any problems you need to eliminate it from your diet completely for at least 2 weeks. After 2-3 weeks you can try to reintroduce it to see how it makes you feel.

Gluten is the protein complex, consisting of glutenins and gliadins, found in wheat, rye and barley, as well as old-fashioned forms of wheat including spelt. Our parents and grandparents may well be bemused by the growing gluten-free 'fad'. But the bread they were eating then and the bread we're eating now is very different.

Modern wheat – a modern poison?

In the 1960s Norman Borlaug won the Nobel Prize for essentially preventing the world from dying of starvation. He genetically modified wheat to produce a new hybrid crop; it was more pest-resistant and had shorter thicker stems which meant it could carry more grain without collapsing. But this new wheat contained more gluten, and a different sort of gluten, than did the traditional crop. In William Davis's opinion, modern wheat is a 'perfect, chronic poison'. Davis is an American cardiologist and author of the New York Times bestseller

Wheat Belly; Lose the Wheat, Lose the Weight, and Find Your Path Back to Health (2014).

Think about the foods you overeat or possibly even binge on. Would these foods include bread? Or pasta or pizza or biscuits or cookies? Do you 'love' bread, do you crave it? Do you feel comforted when you eat it? Cravings for gluten-containing foods can be a sign that they are affecting our brain chemistry. The blood-brain barrier is designed to keep the brain safe from toxins but gliadin, a gluten protein, is small enough to cross the blood-brain barrier and once across it can attach to the opiate receptors.[1]

Drugged-up

Casein, the milk protein, can do the same thing. And when gluten and casein activate the opiate receptors it's like a little morphine hit, which feels pretty good. When we cut these foods out of our diet some of us might experience withdrawal symptoms. Davies has found that about 30% of his patients suffer with fatigue, mental fogginess, irritability or low mood, which generally lasts from 2-5 days.

Bread made with 100% rye is an optional extra from day 16 onwards. It's not a 'health food' and we don't need it but some of us can't imagine a life without bread and rye is better tolerated than wheat. I advise people to have it if they feel they really need it but not to eat it as a matter of course. Farmers have known for years that if they want to fatten up their animals in order to get more money for them at market, they give them grains to eat.

Remember that grains are carbohydrates which break down to sugar and that sugar is readily stored as fat. When you're tempted by bread remember the farmers fattening up their animals for market; grains have the same effect on us, so keep rye, and all grains, to a minimum.

There's another reason not to eat rye as a matter of course. There may be days on the programme that feel difficult. If you're routinely eating rye bread you've got nothing up your sleeve for when you're feeling a bit hard done by. A slice of toasted rye spread with avocado and topped with a poached egg is a cheery sight. Remember it's not important or even necessary to include whole grains as part of a healthy diet and in fact most people do better without them.

To summarise, the no wheat and no grain rule is important because:

- Grains are carbohydrates which break down quickly to sugar and are easily stored as fat
- Grains increase insulin which is pro-inflammatory and which makes us hungry
- Gluten is allergenic and makes the gut leaky
- Wheat makes us hungrier

---

1   Pruimboom, L. & De Punder, K. 2015. The opioid effects of gluten exorphins: asymptomatic celiac disease. *Journal of Health, Population, and Nutrition,* 33:24 Available: https://jhpn.biomedcentral.com/articles/10.1186/s41043-015-0032-y [Accessed 30 September 2018]

- Van Den Broeck, H. C. et al 2010. Presence of celiac disease epitopes in modern and old hexaploid wheat varieties: wheat breeding may have contributed to increased prevalence of celiac disease. TAG. Theoretical and Applied Genetics. Theoretische Und Angewandte Genetik, 121(8)1527-1539. Available: https://link.springer.com/article/10.1007%2Fs00122-010-1408-4 [Accessed 30 September 2018]

Rule 9: No cardio exercise for 16 days

IF YOU'RE ALREADY fit and active and you work out regularly there's no reason not to continue a light version of your regime in Phases 1 and 2. But if you're not especially fit and you've never liked the idea of exercise, chances are that will change. As you lose weight and begin to feel better about yourself you'll be raring to go. But this is not the moment to start.

For some people, being told they are not allowed to exercise for 16 days is music to their ears. But others are horrified and can't imagine not getting up a sweat for two weeks (see the Troubleshooting section and Infrared Sauna). The no exercise rule doesn't mean lying on the sofa for 2 weeks (although that seems to work well too) but it does mean low-intensity exercise only. Walking is positively excellent exercise and a good rule of thumb is that if you can hold a normal conversation, and not get out of breath while you're walking, you're in the safe zone. No panting.

A few years ago I saw a woman in her early 40s who'd sprained her ankle just as she was about to start the programme. She really was forced to lie on the sofa for the first 16 days. She hobbled in to see me before she was due to start Phase 3 and, despite doing zero exercise, she gained muscle and lost fat, purely as a result of changing her diet.

Forest bathing

Leisurely walking as opposed to power walking, and especially in woods or forests, decreases the stress hormone, cortisol. Have a look at the review: *Shinrin-Yoku (Forest Bathing) and Nature Therapy*.[1] But heavy or prolonged cardiovascular exercise increases cortisol because it is perceived by our immune system as a stressor. And we react to stressors as dangers, whether they be lions, traffic wardens or missed trains. These stressors push us into fight or flight mode and increase our stress hormones, which make it harder to lose fat.

Research shows (and most of us are well aware) that we are hungrier and more interested in eating carbs following a 'stressful event'.[2,3] And intense or prolonged exercise counts as a stressful event. Chronically high levels of cortisol can make the body hold onto fat and what we're after, while we're still persuading the body to burn fat rather than sugar for energy, is lower stress and lower cortisol levels. So walking, tai chi and yoga are the exercises to focus on. We do not need to exercise to lose weight, and as we've learned, too much exercise is counter-productive and prevents us from burning fat.

The wrong kind of exercise, just like too much stress, can make us fatter not thinner. In other words, exercise is not just about burning calories; more important is the effect that exercise has on our muscles, hormones and hunger. Heavy exercise is the enemy of fat burning, and it results not only in muscle loss but also more susceptibility to infection and injury.

Muscle burning exercise

The Sunday Times journalist, Mat Rudd, wrote a fascinating article for the paper in July 2017[4] and eloquently makes the case against extreme exercise for overall health and weight loss. His regime, in his quest for perfectly muscled fitness, involved 18 months of '*High-intensity training*.

Treadmills. Boxercise. Hardcore stuff. And a lot of running'. He wrote about his results following a body scan: *'The net result of the past 18 months of sweat, toil and nausea is that I have lost 8kg of body weight — and at least a big chunk of that appears to be the red meat. The vast majority of new classes I've been skipping along to are of the maximum-heart-rate variety. That's the big trend in an industry obsessed with weight loss. The focus is on burning calories, which is why I'm so often the only bloke in the room...I've burnt more calories than I have consumed. I've developed the physique of a malnourished long-distance runner.'*

Rudd had discovered something that many of us have yet to discover – cardio exercise does not burn fat. The myth is that the only way to get thinner is to exercise like a fiend and many of us translate that into meaning that unless we're exercising so hard we feel physically sick, we're not doing enough. Remember the lady who twisted her ankle and who lay on the sofa for 2 weeks – her fat mass decreased and her muscle mass increased purely because of what she was eating. In other words, we can burn the fat and build the muscle with our knife and fork and with no need for track suits or trainers.

Slow burn

Later, once we've lost the fat, of course we'll put the trainers back on and get into a regime that builds strength and fitness, but for now it's walking all the way. Stu Mittelman, an endurance athlete, who once ran 3000 miles from San Diego to New York, co-wrote an excellent book, *'Slow Burn – Burn fat faster by exercising slower' (2000).* As he explains, to burn fat we need to keep our heart rate down; if we're exercising too hard we're just burning sugar for energy. The more sugar our body burns the less fat it burns. Tony Robbins, who's always strived to be the best he could be, wrote the foreword, in which he said: *'With Stu's guidance, I achieved the outcomes of a peak physical state and endless energy and enjoyed the process'.* Persuading your body to make the switch from burning carbs for energy to burning fat for energy can take a couple of weeks. During this time, it's possible or even likely, that you'll feel more tired as your body switches to the new energy source, i.e. stored fat in the body.

For now, the key is to reduce stress – to allow us to get the hormonal reset that we need. We need to move out of fight or flight mode and spend more time in parasympathetic mode – this is the rest and repair part of the nervous system. The sympathetic nervous system is the accelerator and the parasympathetic is the brakes. So even if you're super fit consider taking a couple of weeks out from your normal routine – go for walks, get to bed earlier and rest up, and you will become a much more efficient fat-burner.

Some people, being devoted disciples of the dogma that weight loss is impossible without exercise, have felt unable to follow the no exercise rule. Despite the advice, and the lack of energy they felt, they carried on exercising, and witnessed a decrease in both muscle mass and metabolic rate. They also saw an *increase* in body fat and sometimes even visceral fat too (visceral fat is the dangerous fat that accumulates around the organs). There's nothing in our repertoire to protect us against chronic over-exercising and undereating. When we are exercising too hard, the body breaks down the proteins in our muscles and turns them into sugar to keep us going. The kind of exercise that some of us are putting ourselves through is counter-survival; our muscles are good for occasional sprints but they're better adapted, evolutionarily speaking, for long walks and lifting heavy objects like logs.

What should I eat before exercising?

People often ask me what they should eat before they exercise. And the answer is always the same. Nothing! In our caveman days if we were hungry or thirsty we had to take to our feet to find the solution. And when we exercise on an empty stomach not only are we switching to fat-burning mode but we're also reducing inflammation and growing our brain. Read Leo Pruimboom's fascinating 2015 paper '*Physical*

Activity Protects the Human Brain against Metabolic Stress Induced by a Postprandial and Chronic Inflammation' to find out more.[5]

Get a walk in before lunch, even if it's just for 10 minutes outside, it will be positively good for you. Walking increases our stomach acid, which we need to digest our food, but extreme exercise decreases it. That makes sense – extreme exercise switches on fight or flight and is the enemy of digestion. Walking, as well as improving digestion, has anti-inflammatory effects and even stimulates the growth of friendly microbes in the gut.[6] Always exercise before you eat. There is no question that exercise is vitally important for our physical and mental health and overall wellbeing, but for 2 weeks, 16 days to be exact, just walk.

We've learned that eating breakfast within an hour of waking helps to reset our body clock, our circadian rhythm. If you can get to work within an hour of waking up, do this: incorporate exercise during the week by taking breakfast to work with you. Get off the tube or bus a stop or two before you need to and eat breakfast when you arrive. If it takes you longer than an hour to get from bed to work, breakfast before you go.

To summarise, the reasons for the no cardio exercise rule are:

- You are trying to persuade your body to make the switch from burning carbohydrates (sugar) for energy to burning fat for energy.

- Too much exercise too soon can result in muscle loss because it's easier for the body to burn muscle rather than fat.

- Heavy exercise can make us hungrier and particularly hungry for high carb foods

- You're not taking in enough calories to fuel heavy exercise and you're not eating enough protein for muscle repair and rebuilding

- Heavy exercise is a stressor which results in higher levels of cortisol (and we know that too much cortisol makes us fat)

1   Hansen, M. M., Jones, R. & Tocchini, K. 2017. Shinrin-Yoku (Forest Bathing) and Nature Therapy: A State-of-the- Art Review. International Journal of Environmental Research and Public Health, 14(8):851. Available:https://www.mdpi.com/1660-4601/14/8/851/htm [Accessed 30 September 2018]

2   Epel, E., Lapidus, R., Mcewen, B. & Brownell, K. 2001. Stress may add bite to appetite in women: a laboratory study of stress-induced cortisol and eating behavior. Psychoneuroendocrinology, 26(1):37-49

3   Ans, A et al 2018. Neurohormonal Regulation of Appetite and its Relationship with Stress: A Mini Literature Review. Cureus 10(7): e3032. Available: https://www.cureus.com/articles/13630-neurohormonal-regulation-of-appetite-and-its-relationship-with-stress-a-mini-literature-review [Accessed 10 October 2018]

4   Rudd, M. 2017. Body: Help! High-intensity training burnt off my muscles [Online]. The Sunday Times. Available: https://www.thetimes.co.uk/article/matt-rudd-high-intensity-training-burnt-off-my-muscles-whxlq7pmk [Accessed 30 September 2018].

5   Pruimboom, L., Raison, C.L., Muskiet, F.A.J 2015. Physical Activity Protects the Human Brain against Metabolic Stress Induced by a Postprandial and Chronic Inflammation. Behavioural Neurology, 2015: 569869. Available: https://www.hindawi.com/journals/bn/2015/569869/ [Accessed 30 September 2018]

6   Monda, V et al 2017. Exercise Modifies the Gut Microbiota with Positive Health Effects. Oxidative Medicine and Cellular Longevity, 2017, 3831972. Available: https://www.hindawi.com/journals/omcl/2017/3831972/ [Accessed 30 September 2018]

Rule 10: No Sugar (and no honey or stevia or fake sugars)

MOST OF US have experienced the roller coaster of blood sugar highs and lows. When we're feeling a bit tired and in need of an energy boost it's tempting to reach for something sweet, which quickly raises our energy and our blood sugar. Sugar levels shoot up and lots of insulin is produced; the insulin does a great job of taking the sugar out of the blood and pulling it into the cells, where it can be burned for energy or stored as fat. We need B vitamins to make stomach acid but we also need them (along with vitamin C, magnesium and zinc) to deal with the sugar that we eat. Eating sugar depletes these nutrients, which are the very ones we need for making energy. Ultimately, sugar exhausts us.

But sometimes insulin does too good a job and blood sugar falls too fast; it can fall to a lower level than it was before we had the snack.[1] And with low blood sugar comes hunger and the whole cycle starts again – we look for our next sugar fix. But eating regular meals and combining protein with vegetables means that hunger, and peaks and troughs in energy, quickly become a thing of the past. If we keep eating carbs and sugar we can't expect our body to be able to make the switch from burning sugar to burning fat for energy.

The selfish brain

Putting something sweet into our mouth affects two separate organs: the brain, and the pancreas, which, as we know releases insulin. The hypothalamus in the brain equates that sweet taste with energy. And in our evolutionary history, aeons before we could synthesise fake sweeteners like aspartame, sweetness was a signal to the brain that it could safely release energy to the rest of the body because its own energy needs were about to be met. The sweeter the taste, the stronger the signal to the brain to expect energy.

One of the reasons that people who drink zero-calorie drinks are more inclined to put on weight, is the effect those fake sweeteners have on the brain. The brain, sometimes referred to as the 'selfish brain'[2] picks up on the sweet taste, and is fooled into allocating energy to the rest of the body. But when the brain fails to get the expected energy after all, it sends us searching for food. That means that those fake sugars increase our appetite and make us fat. And they also have a devastating effect on our friendly microbes and may well set the scene for insulin resistance too.[3,4]

Fat and wrinkly

Personally, if I'm tempted by something sweet, I say to myself *'yes of course you can have that but just remember that it will make you fat and wrinkly'* and that usually does the trick; no thanks. It's not just sugar that makes us fat and wrinkly – the other culprits are bread, rice, pastry, biscuits, cakes, and potatoes, because they all break down into sugar in our blood. That sugar is not only stored as fat but it also results in 'stiffer' skin, i.e. wrinkles. I hope that helps to put you off? How does sugar result in stiffer skin? It's a process called glycation[5,6] in which sugar changes the structure of proteins and fats, resulting in 'advanced glycation end products' (AGEs) which damage our tendons, arteries, bones, muscles and skin. AGEs - an easy acronym to remember.

To summarise, the reasons for the no sugar/honey/fake sweeteners rule is to help us:

- Maintain steady blood sugar and insulin levels

- Keep hunger under control
- Keep inflammation and ageing at bay
- Protect our microbes
- Help our body make the switch from sugar burning to fat burning

The Hedgehog – a cautionary tale

Picture the hedgehog emerging from his burrow in the spring. He's thin and he's hungry after spending all winter hibernating. He goes out to forage for his favourite foods which are naturally high in protein: insects, slugs and worms, and the occasional baby mouse. He has a terrific spring and summer, gets married, and has a few babies. All goes well until the autumn; the colder days mean his usual supply of food all but disappears. But fruit – apples and berries – start falling to the ground and, feeling hungry, he takes a couple of tentative bites.

The fruit sugar hits his blood stream quickly, and this is followed by the release of lots of insulin. His blood sugar crashes and the hedgehog feels hungry and maybe even a bit shaky. He has another couple of bites of fruit; his blood sugar soars, more insulin is produced, his blood sugar crashes. The cycle is repeated again and again.

And we all know what happens. With the high levels of blood sugar and insulin, the hedgehog gets fatter and fatter and eventually, once he's accumulated enough fat to hibernate, he crawls into his burrow for the winter. And that's a great survival tactic for the hedgehog but it's not so good for us. We don't want any sugar spikes, or ravenous hunger; we're eating 3 times a day and combining protein with vegetables, which results in stable blood sugar and low insulin levels, which allows us to burn fat and to reset our hormones.

1   Castro, R. 2016. Reactive hypoglycemia: What can I do? [Online]. Mayo Foundation for Medical Education and Research. Available: https://www.mayoclinic.org/diseases-conditions/diabetes/expert-answers/reactive-hypoglycemia/faq-20057778 [Accessed 30 September 2018].

2 Peters, A., Kubera, B., Hubold, C. & Langemann, D. 2011. The Selfish Brain: Stress and Eating Behavior. Frontiers in Neuroscience, 5, 74. Available: https://www.frontiersin.org/articles/10.3389/fnins.2011.00074/full [Accessed 30 September 2018]

3 Nettleton, J. E., Reimer, R. A. & Shearer, J. 2016. Reshaping the gut microbiota: Impact of low calorie sweeteners and the link to insulin resistance? Physiology & Behavior, 164, 488-493.

4 Mosdøl, A et al 2018. Hypotheses and evidence related to intense sweeteners and effects on appetite and body weight changes: A scoping review of reviews. PLoS ONE 13(7): e0199558. Available: https://journals.plos.org/plosone/article?id=10.1371/journal.pone.0199558 [Accessed 10 October 2018]

5 Clatici, V. G. et al 2017. Perceived Age and Life Style. The Specific Contributions of Seven Factors Involved in Health and Beauty. Maedica, 12(3)191-201. Available: https://www.ncbi.nlm.nih.gov/pmc/articles/PMC5706759/ [Accessed 30 September 2018]

6 Fournet, M., Bonté, F. and Desmoulière, A. 2018. Glycation Damage: A Possible Hub for Major Pathophysiological Disorders and Aging. *Aging and disease*, 9(5), p.880. Available: https://www.ncbi.nlm.nih.gov/pmc/articles/PMC6147582/ [Accessed 10 October 2018]

PART 3

1: The mind set

IT GOES WITHOUT saying that succeeding with any new project requires preparation as well as commitment. The more you think about the programme before you start, and the better you plan it, the more likely you are to succeed. So that means looking at your diary and finding 16 clear days, free of social or business commitments that involve eating or drinking. Meeting friends for dinner is obviously out, unless you're in the kitchen, but drinks are easier. Sparkling water, ice and a slice of lemon is perfect and no one will know that it's not gin and tonic. If you absolutely have to go out for a meal in the first 16 days, a little white lie won't go amiss. Tell the waiters that you are on a 'medical programme' and must avoid oil. And tell them if your food is cooked with oil you'll have to send it back to the kitchen. That does the trick.

Start by thinking about all the reasons you'd like to feel better and lose weight, or get your skin or digestive issues sorted. A time-sensitive goal always helps to focus us, perhaps a wedding, a birthday, or a holiday for which you'd like to look and feel your best. Or maybe you've got a wardrobe full of clothes that are just too small. Then write down how achieving that goal weight will make you feel; include as much detail as possible and really allow yourself to feel the new confidence, the lightness, and the pride at being back in control. See and feel yourself in the clothes you'd like to wear; imagine standing in front of a mirror and smiling back at yourself, delighted with your reflection. It might sound silly but this visualisation is key.

And practice feeling that amazing feeling *now*, not in 3 months' time. Our subconscious mind is powerful. If we keep saying to ourselves

'I'm too fat/I look gross /I'll never succeed, we are constantly giving our subconscious the message that this is what we most want, because this is what we're focusing on.

Emotional eating

Many of us, especially women, are emotional eaters; we eat to change the way we feel, whether we're bored or broken-hearted. But without recourse to snacks and our former tactic of using food to distract us, we have to face our emotions head-on, and that can be painful. Expect to feel emotional as you go through the process – it's completely normal. Losing weight is a bit like peeling an onion – as we lose weight the emotions that we experienced when we were overeating, or eating junk, are liable to resurface. Eating to change the way we feel rather than eating because we're hungry is emotional eating. Our feelings get stuffed back down and swallowed as food. Ultimately, we need to process the feelings and the best way to do that is not by eating but by writing.

2: Writing to heal

ARE THERE MEMORIES of experiences in your past that still make you feel sad, angry, hurt, or resentful? For most of us, that's likely to be the case. We may experience, especially when we're children, stressful or traumatic events which we feel unable to share with anyone. And the resulting unexpressed emotions remain inside us, gently festering away. Unresolved stress and hurt from the past activates not the fight or flight pathway, which is for life-threatening danger, but the hypothalamus-pituitary-adrenal (HPA) system. The HPA is activated by stress and trauma and may remain stuck in the 'on' position[1] for years.

The experiences of the past might still be affecting us both physically and emotionally and sapping our energy. Signs of this can manifest as low self-esteem, addiction, anxiety or depression and all kinds of chronic physical problems from overweight to acne rosacea to IBS. We can switch off the HPA activation by processing and coming to terms with the experiences of our past. Writing is one of the ways in which we can process these feelings.

Have a look at the work of John Sarno and James Pennebaker – both have studied and written about the powerful effects of writing on physical and emotional healing. Get into the habit of writing for at least ten minutes (twenty minutes would be even better) every day. Write about anything that makes you feel emotional. Read what you've written once and throw it away. If you don't plan to throw the paper away you can't really express what needs to be expressed in case somebody else finds it and reads it.

Adverse childhood experiences: ACEs

Our parents may not have brought us up in a way that made us feel safe and loved. They may have treated us as their parents treated them - still believing that their parents knew best. As little children, we regard our parents as perfect beings and if they are angry with us, or shout at us, or ignore us, or even hit us, we blame ourselves. In our eyes they are perfect, so it must be our fault, we are the guilty ones, not them. Even little children know that baddies must be punished and it's the anticipation of the punishment that keeps us on high alert – our HPA stress system is chronically activated.

It was on Leo's cPNI course where I learned about both writing as therapy, and 'Adverse childhood experiences' or ACEs.[2] Regretfully I never had a great relationship with my dad and although he died a few years ago I was still angry with him. I didn't want to be angry; I knew that for both of us I needed to forgive him but I didn't know how. So I followed Leo's advice and wrote my dad a letter. I was shocked by what came up and by the emotions that surfaced. But once I'd let the anger out and accused him, I could begin to understand him and then to forgive him. It felt as if a huge weight had been lifted from me; I felt more energetic and happier in my skin. And now, when he pops into my head, I think of the good things he did for me, and the lessons he taught me for which I'm grateful. All thanks to a letter written to him after he had died.

1   Godoy, L. D. et al 2018. A Comprehensive Overview on Stress Neurobiology: Basic Concepts and Clinical Implications. Frontiers in Behavioral Neuroscience, 12, 127. Available: https://www.frontiersin.org/articles/10.3389/fnbeh.2018.00127/full [Accessed 30 September 2018]

2   Hughes, K., et al 2017. The effect of multiple adverse childhood experiences on health: a systematic review and meta-analysis. The Lancet Public Health, 2(8) e356-e366. Available: https://www.thelancet.com/journals/lanpub/article/PIIS2468-2667(17)30118-4/fulltext [Accessed 30 September 2018]

•   Sarno, J. E. 2007. The Divided Mind: The Epidemic of Mindbody Disorders, New York, NY, HarperCollins.

•   Sarno, J. E. 2010. Healing Back Pain: The Mind-Body Connection, New York, NY, Grand Central Publishing.

- Pennebaker, J. W. 2004. Writing to Heal: A Guided Journal for Recovering from Trauma and Emotional Upheaval, New York, NY, New Harbinger Publications.

3: Practical advice

NEARLY EVERYONE, WHEN starting the programme, is frightened of feeling hungry. Odd though it sounds, you are likely to find that reconnecting with the feeling of actual hunger is strangely satisfying. Following the programme forces us to become more mindful eaters. When I first took myself through the MB programme I felt like an angry dog jealously guarding its food. At mealtimes, I didn't want to talk to anyone, I wanted to focus on eating.

In the Mayr clinics, they encourage their patients to sit, silent as Carmelite nuns, while they're eating. And I understand why – when we wolf down our food, we hardly experience it. Just look at the way a dog swallows a treat, he barely chews it and maybe doesn't even taste it. Years ago I remember sharing some sweets with my mother's dog. I gave her a Malteser (a small round chocolate) and watched in horror as she swallowed the whole thing – I traced it going down her little throat. I was so grateful that it did go down and didn't get stuck, I loved that dog.

On this programme there's not very much food; the portions will possibly look small to you when you start, and because you're only eating 3 times a day you might as well be conscious of what you're doing and get some pleasure while you're at it. Honour yourself by laying a nice place at the table, and make everything look appetising and appealing.

Women are used to looking after everyone else and generally put themselves at the bottom of the to do list with the lowest priority.

Following this programme means we have to do a certain amount of self-nurturing. I remember coming home from work one day feeling hungry and exhausted. I stood over the kitchen counter picking at a leftover roast chicken and having a bite or two of the cold vegetables. And as I stood there I thought to myself 'what would I do if my husband came in from work and he was tired and hungry? Would I say to him 'there's a chicken over there, go and pick away at it?" No of course not. I'd cut some slices for him, put them on a plate with the vegetables that I'd heated up, and make it look appetising. And that's what we need to do for ourselves.

Practical advice – these are the things to equip yourself with before you start:

- Digital scales for weighing out your food portions
- Tape measure to keep track of your measurements
- Tupperware containers for meals on the go
- Water filter
- Pint glasses to keep track of your water
- Food diary (but you can equally well use your phone)
- Writing pad
- Epsom salts
- A spiralizer to make vegetables more fun

PART 4: The 4 phases of the programme

MUCH LIKE MANY other programmes, including Dukan and Atkins, this one is split into 4 phases. Remember that even though a lot of the information here relates to weight loss, what we are aiming for is the metabolic reset, and the rebalancing of our hormones and our rhythm, and the side effect of that is weight loss. Here they are again:

1. Phase 1 **Prep**: 2 days - lots of vegetables

2. Phase 2 **Reset**: 14 days —strict; weighing all food, no oil/ grains/ sugar/ alcohol

3. Phase 3 **Burn**: 10 weeks – or until goal weight is reached. Oil is reintroduced; and a weekly treat meal

4. Phase 4 **Forever**

It's the liver which is crucially involved in fat-burning, and just to recap, two of the liver's other biggest tasks are detoxification and fat digestion. The first sixteen days, Phase 1 and Phase 2, are oil and alcohol-free, so this could be described as a liver holiday and it allows this organ to get down to some serious fat burning. One of the signs of a sluggish liver, is fat accumulation around the tummy along with a pot belly. Or a little (or large) roll of fat develops around the upper abdomen, fondly termed a "liver roll". It's hard to lose this abdominal fat until liver function is improved. But once the liver's been given some time off and some TLC it starts to burn fat more efficiently again and the belly fat melts away.

The first 16 days are sacrosanct

The first 16 days must be treated as sacrosanct because it is this period that seems to act as a metabolic reset. In Phase 2, we're reminding the body about how to use stored fat rather than sugar as an energy source. In practice, I've noticed that when this induction time is interrupted or not completed in 16 straight days nothing works as it should and ultimately people don't get the results they want. That's why I frighten people a bit with the idea of having to start again if they break the rules. Most people find it a challenging 2 weeks but knowing that successful completion of this phase is setting the scene for victory makes it easier.

Finding support, ideally from a coach if you can afford to, or failing that a good friend, is invaluable. A little friendly competition can be a great motivator too. Support yourself by doing the writing, and of course being super prepared. Keep reminding yourself why you're doing this. Keep revisiting the reasons you wanted to lose weight or to feel better in the first place. Write the reasons on your phone and read them first thing every morning to set yourself up for a successful day. And take it one day at a time.

The most dramatic weight loss usually occurs in the first 16 days and that's just as well as it helps get you through the toughest part of the programme. A quick win early on is both inspiring and rewarding. Although much of this weight loss may well be water, the difference you are likely to see on the scales, as well as in the mirror, inspires and eggs you on. It does happen, but thankfully rarely, that there's a modest weight loss of only 3 or 4 pounds in the first 2 weeks. But take cheer in the fact that you won't be behind for long. Naturally we all like to know what to expect – how much we're going to lose and how quickly. The answer is that we all lose weight at different rates but the average weight loss over 3 months is 2-3 pounds a week. Generally speaking, the more weight you've got to lose, the faster it initially comes off.

Your vital statistics

Before you start the programme take your measurements. Get a tape measure and measure your waist around the tummy button, and then measure around the widest part of your hips, and around the widest part of your left thigh, and write it down. This is important because occasionally the overall weight doesn't change in some weeks but the measurements do. That typically happens when people are replacing fat with muscle. Your fat mass is decreasing because you're sticking to the programme. But when you're eating more protein than you're used to, you're also building muscle, and muscle is heavier than fat. If you don't take your measurements and you haven't got an accurate body composition analyser at home, to check your fat, muscle and water percentages, you're likely to get despondent if it looks as if nothing is happening on the scales.

Try not to weigh yourself every day – much better to save it for a Saturday or Sunday morning. Our weight naturally fluctuates from day to day, depending on how much water we've drunk and how much salt we've had, because salt can result in water retention. Even if you don't add salt to your food, remember that foods like cheese and smoked salmon contain a lot of it. And one more thing to consider is how 'regular' you are. Even my fancy scales can't tell how much of your overall weight might be sitting in your bowels. See constipation in Troubleshooting if this is an issue for you.

Phase 3 begins on day 17 and this is when life becomes much easier and more normal again. Because you've been weighing out your food portions for the past 16 days you've got a pretty good idea of what the right sized portion looks like. And because this is also when oil is reintroduced you can eat out in restaurants and still follow the rules easily. And, best of all you get to have a treat meal once a week when you break all the rules and have a feast. Even if you're not using the programme to lose weight, for best results stay in this phase for 10 weeks before moving into the forever phase.

Phase 4, this starts when you have reached your target weight, or if you are not following the programme for weight loss, at the end of the twelfth week. You might be surprised to find that some of the foods you thought you could never live without, things like butter or sugar, or crisps, or wheat, just don't enter your consciousness anymore; either because you've found they don't make you feel so well or just because your taste buds have changed. But if you still fancy those foods that's fine, you can still enjoy them now and then.

1: Phase 1 – Preparation Phase

How to do it

MANY FIND THE first 2 days the hardest part of the programme – mainly because they've gone cold turkey on wheat, dairy, alcohol and sugar and the body goes into full detox mode. You might get headaches or feel you're coming down with flu; you might feel tired. But you might not feel any of these symptoms at all and you'll just sail through it looking forward to some more interesting food on day 3. Nevertheless, it's a good idea to do these 2 days when you're at home rather than at work.

Preparation is a 2-day vegetable fast – no oil, no alcohol, no sugar, and no fruit or grains, just vegetables. Vegetables provide minerals and great amounts of fibre which is not only beloved by our friendly microbes but which also helps to keep us feeling fuller for longer. During these 2 days focus on eating vegetables which are grown above ground: green beans, broccoli, cauliflower, cabbage, artichokes, asparagus, squash, courgettes, celery – but a few root vegetables including carrots, sweet potato and beetroot are fine.

And you can count avocado, given its low sugar content, and tomato, as vegetables too. But sweet corn and pulses (peas, lentils, kidney beans, chick peas etc.) don't count as vegetables and must be avoided in this phase. Potato is out too. Artichoke hearts, bottled in brine rather than oil, are delicious and filling. Liberal use of chilli, ginger and garlic, if you like the taste, and fresh, frozen or dried herbs, sea salt and pepper, are all fine.

Aim for about ½ kilo (1 pound) of vegetables per meal but quantity is not so important at this stage – if that feels too much have less and if it doesn't feel enough have more. Try having avocado and tomato for breakfast with a few basil leaves, salt and pepper and some apple cider vinegar.

It doesn't matter how you prepare the vegetables as long as you don't use any oil or fat. You'll probably find that a combination of soup (see Recipes) steamed vegetables and salads with avocado and raw vegetables like fennel, and lots of herbs will make the meals more interesting. You can also make some vegetable smoothies with fresh vegetable stock and a mixture of vegetables but avoid juicing them because the fibre is all important for the microbes and for your detox.

Start day 1 with 3 teaspoons of Epsom salts, 30 minutes or longer before breakfast. They taste awful but you only need take them once. Stir them into half a glass of warm water until they've dissolved, add cold water and drink. Then drink lots more water to take the taste away. The salts act as a laxative (another reason to do this at home rather that at work) and can result in a dramatic evacuation but everyone reacts to them differently. You definitely don't want to take the salts before setting off on the school run, or on your commute; happily, the worst of it is normally over by lunchtime.

Do remember to drink lots of water in the first two days. You can drink black or green tea or coffee, with or between meals in your first 2 days and you don't need to worry about the 5 hour fast between meals until day 3.

Additional notes for the Preparation Phase

No lab food

As discussed, the vegetables can be eaten raw or steamed and they can also be made into soup using fresh stock, which can be homemade or bought at the supermarket, but stock cubes are out. Why no stock cubes? Here are the ingredients of a well-known company's vegetable stock cube: *Salt, vegetable fats (palm, shea, sal), potato starch, yeast extract, sugar, onion powder, carrots, herbs, spices, tomato powder, red pepper, caramel syrup, flavourings, leek, maltodextrin.* What we're aiming for on the programme is whole foods which have been minimally processed, we don't want added sugars or artificial flavourings which have been conjured up in a lab. Here are the ingredients in a well-known brand's liquid stock: *Water, onion extract, broccoli extract, carrot extract, celery extract, spinach extract, parsley, tarragon, dried sage, garlic purée, ground bay leaf, ground thyme, ground white pepper.* Much better. Chicken stock/broth can be substituted for vegetable stock.

Vegetables – microbe heaven

Vegetables feed the friendly microbes which are vital to our health, and optimally we need both high numbers and a high diversity of these creatures. Each microbe has its own favourite fibre so if we only eat carrots and broccoli we're only feeding a very few species. So be brave, try vegetables you've never tried before, your microbes will love you for it and will work even harder to keep you well. Further down you'll find a list of vegetables to inspire you. And include as many herbs as you can, including basil, sage, rosemary, thyme, garlic, tarragon, chives, ginger, and chilli, to make your meals more interesting and to make them even more nutritious.

2: Phase 2 – Reset

How to do it

AS ALREADY MENTIONED, the first 16 days need to be treated as sacro-sanct because it's this 16-day period that acts as a metabolic reset in the body. When people don't complete the first 16 days consecutively they don't get the reset. Eating protein food again, like eggs and fish comes as a welcome relief on day 3, and you're likely to notice in the first few days that your taste buds have changed – everything tastes more interesting again.

Remember that you are grain-free, oil-free, alcohol-free and sugar-free for the next 14 days. It's during this phase that you're communicating metabolically with your body and changing it from a sugar burner into a fat-burning machine. Energy can dip during the first few days of this phase – it's as if the body is saying *'Give me food I've got no fuel here'* And you're saying, *'We're going to be burning fat for energy now, no more sugar'* and the body's reply is *'I don't know how to do that'*. But it does make the switch and it's almost palpable, and with that your energy returns – not just back to normal though, you'll find that it's better than it has been for ages.

In the first few days, as your body searches for fuel, it's in semi-starvation mode and the metabolic rate drops. The usual supply of carbs has dried up, and the body's forgotten how to access its fat stores for energy, so we burn a bit of muscle. The proteins in our muscle can be broken down to sugar for the body to use as energy. But if we are also exercising at this point, the muscle loss is amplified. Hence the no exercise rule in phase 2 – you want to keep your muscles intact and focus on burning fat for energy.

Change your go-to breakfast

If yoghurt and fruit was your go-to breakfast and you were used to having a snack at about 11am, give yourself a break and try something else for a couple of weeks and see how you feel. Make a note of the time you had breakfast and what time you felt hungry again – if you're starving after a couple of hours it means you've had a blood sugar crash. Your sugar has risen too fast, you've produced too much insulin and now your blood sugar is too low.

If you weigh between 50-75kgs use the weights below – if you weigh 76-100kgs add 10g more vegetables and 10g more protein per meal. If you weigh over 100kg add 20g of each to the weights below, and if you're having eggs as the protein for your meal, eat 3.

- 160g unsweetened unflavoured full-fat sheep, cow or goat yoghurt with 100g of one type of fruit – e.g. 100g berries
- 2 eggs with 100g any vegetables, e.g. spinach, courgette and mushrooms
- 6 teaspoons (35g) of pumpkin and sunflower seeds with 100g vegetables
- 100g chicken or turkey with 100g vegetables
- 100g fish, e.g. salmon (or a kipper!) with 100g vegetables
- 75g smoked salmon with 100g vegetables (less weight for smoked salmon than fresh as it contains less water)

Vegetables for breakfast?

Vegetables for breakfast? Why not! Remember that avocado and tomato count as vegetables here – they're delicious and of course require no cooking. In the meal planner below you'll see the vegetable weight is 100g – you can have up to 80g avocado per meal, so 80g of the breakfast vegetable weight could be avocado, along with 20g tomato. If you have avocado for breakfast you might want to avoid having it for other meals. Not because it's unhealthy but because you'll get sick of it and won't even want it for breakfast (believe me it's a common complaint) which can make life more difficult. Here are some breakfast examples:

2 eggs	6 teaspoons (35g) sunflower & pumpkin seeds	100g chicken or turkey breast (no skin)
100g vegetables	100g vegetables or 1 apple	100g vegetables

75g smoked salmon	160g full fat cow, sheep or goat yoghurt	100g fresh salmon
100g vegetables	1 type of fruit	100g vegetables

Phase 2 Breakfast

Scandinavians routinely breakfast on fish, meat or cheese whereas most of us in the UK are more inclined to opt for what we feel are traditional breakfast foods, including porridge, cereal, fruit juice and toast. But that traditional weekday breakfast, of high carb, high sugar foods is the worst way to start the day.

Breakfast biscuits? Might as well eat any kind of biscuits, or cocoa pops for that matter; they're packed full of sugar and are likely to raise blood sugar quickly, which then crashes and leaves you starving an hour or two later. But eating protein for breakfast, especially when combined with some vegetables, keeps blood sugar and energy stable for hours. Historically, one of our favourite breakfasts was kippers, and a kipper with vegetables such as mushrooms and tomato makes a great meal.

Some of us can eat porridge in the morning and it keeps us going all day. Others, me included, eat porridge and we're starving 2 hours later. Same thing with yoghurt and fruit; it suits some of us but others are hungry again soon afterwards. If you like the idea of yoghurt and fruit, try it and see. If it doesn't keep you going for a good few hours, go for one of the other choices the next morning. Eggs, chicken or fish are the best option as they're the highest in protein, which is satiating and satisfying.

You'll notice, on the breakfast examples, that there is no sign of porridge or granola. That doesn't mean that you can never have cereals again, by all means try them, if you would like to, when you move into phase 3. See how they make you feel. Oats are a great source of fibre, which feeds our microbes, and some people do very well on them. Questions to ask yourself after eating them include: How's my energy? Do they keep me going, or am I hungry after a couple of hours? Do they make me bloated?

Phase 2 Lunch and Dinner

Lunch/Dinner	Lunch/Dinner	Lunch/Dinner
130g seafood	130g fish	130g turkey or chicken breast (no skin)
130g vegetables	130g vegetables	130g vegetables

Lunch/Dinner	Lunch/Dinner	Lunch/Dinner
130g meat or 80g cheese	160g pulses (80g dried weight)	100g Tempeh (fermented soy protein)
130g vegetables	130g vegetables	130g vegetables

Food list

Protein Foods	Remember the protein rule – 1 type of protein per meal
Fish – fresh or smoked; Tuna: canned in water or fresh in phase 2	Any, including Cod, Haddock, Halibut, Mackerel, Plaice, Red Mullet, Salmon, Fresh Sardines, Sea Bass, Sea Bream, Skate, Snapper, Sole, Tilapia, Trout, Tuna, Turbot
Poultry	Chicken, Turkey, or Duck breast (no skin in phase 2)
Seafood	Clams, Crab, Lobster, Mussels, Prawns/Shrimps, Squid
Red Meat	Twice a week max –Beef, Lamb or Venison
Pulses	Lentils, Chickpeas, Cannellini/Butter beans/Haricot beans
Seeds	Sunflower and Pumpkin seeds (breakfast only) ground or whole
Eggs	Organic, up to 14 per week (you can replace the protein at lunch or dinner with 2 eggs if you didn't have eggs for breakfast)
Soy	Tofu or Tempeh (fermented soy protein)
Yoghurt	Full-fat, sheep, cow or goat
Cheese	Any non-processed cheese including Cheddar, Gruyere, Mozzarella, Sheep or Goat cheese

Vegetables	
No sweet corn No potato Sweet potato, peppers and beetroot can be reintroduced in phase 3 Aim to include 3 different vegetables with each meal	Artichokes (fresh or bottled in brine in Phase 1 & 2), Asparagus, Aubergine, Avocado *(up to 80g per meal)*, Broccoli, Brussels sprouts, Butternut squash, Cabbage, Carrots, Cauliflower, Celeriac, Celery, Chicory, Chinese leaf lettuce, Courgette/zucchini, Cress, Cucumber, Endive, Fennel, Gherkins (sugar-free), Green beans, Kale, Kohlrabi, Leek, Lettuce (all, including iceberg, romaine, lamb's lettuce), Mushrooms, Okra, Olives, Onions, Pak Choi, Parsnip, Radishes, Rocket, Romanesco, Salsify, Samphire, Seaweed, Shallots, Spring onions, Spinach, Tomato
Fruit – Remember to have 1 apple with one meal. Lemon can be squeezed over fish or chicken	Apple x1. Keep other fruit, including Blueberries, Blackberries, Grapes, Mango, Papaya, Plum, Raspberries, Strawberries to a maximum of 100g per meal

Avocado is limited by weight because it's calorific and we want to keep calories down in this phase (as mentioned before). Up to 80g avocado per meal is fine (with the breakfast proviso mentioned earlier) and make up the weight with other vegetables on the list. Avoid eating a mono diet of vegetables; remember that your microbes love a variety of vegetables and herbs which increases their diversity. Aim for a combination of 3 or more different vegetables per meal. That could mean a combination of lettuce, fennel and carrot for example as salad vegetables, or broccoli, artichoke, and mushrooms for when you want your vegetables cooked.

Use a spiralizer to make vegetables more interesting. You may be wondering why vegetables, which are low in calories and so good for us, are limited. The answer is that they are carbohydrates and remember that carbohydrates break down to sugar, which is easily stored as fat. So keep the vegetables weights and the protein weights within a meal at a 1:1 ratio.

It's important to weigh out your meals during these 2 weeks and to combine equal weights of protein foods and vegetables. But after a few days, begin to test yourself by estimating the weights of the foods, then put them on the scales to check – that's a great way to get your eye in. Ideally you'd weigh the foods before you cook them.

Cooking Tips

You don't need a recipe book to follow the programme and most recipes can be adapted by using vegetable or chicken stock/broth, when they call for oil. But there are a few recipes at the back of the book to get you started. You don't need to do any fancy cooking. You can simply grill a fillet of fish or chicken and steam a selection of vegetables and you can season your food with herbs and spices. And if you don't feel like cooking you can open a packet of prawns and a bag of salad. You can buy tinned or ready-cooked fish, or rotisserie chicken at the supermarket, and eat it with salad or vegetables which don't need to be cooked.

For cooking in the oil free phase, buy yourself a non-toxic, non-stick pan, such as Green Pan https://www.greenpan.co.uk so that you can dry-fry foods. And make sure you have supplies of liquid vegetable or chicken stock/broth so that you can use it to make quasi stir-fries.

Additional Notes for Phase 2

Automatic pilot

Some of us find it easier to keep to a monotonous diet because we don't want to spend much time thinking about what we'll eat – it's easier to run on automatic pilot. It's fine to have chicken for lunch every day, or fish for dinner every night, if the vegetables are varied.

Preparation is the key to success – make yourself a meal planner each week. So you're not thinking to yourself 'it's Tuesday, what do I feel like having?' You'll know that on Tuesday for example, you're going to have eggs, avocado and a couple of cherry tomatoes for breakfast, salmon with green beans, cabbage and broccoli for lunch, and chicken breast with artichoke, mushrooms and salad for dinner. Factor on taking lunch in to work with you – easy options are hard boiled eggs, or smoked salmon or cooked prawns with salad, cooked and cooled green beans, and fennel. To save time, cook extra vegetables and boil your eggs while you're preparing your dinner the night before.

Remember the reason for the 'one type of protein per meal' rule is so that the protein you eat is better absorbed. Have a look at the food list where you can see all the proteins listed. You wouldn't have seeds with yoghurt for example because they are 2 different types of protein. Avoid having the same protein at each meal – it doesn't matter so much for fish, because it's so good for us, but eating chicken 3 times a day is less good. Fish and seafood are in separate categories, so having salmon for lunch and prawns for dinner for example, is fine.

Fruit can make us hungry

Fruit is limited because it's higher in sugar and lower in fibre then vegetables and can make us feel hungrier. In fact some people find that eating their daily apple mid-meal, rather than at the end, keeps them going for longer without hunger pangs – try making the first and last bite of your meal a protein food. Remember that the only compulsory fruit is the magic apple. If you wanted to keep fruit to a minimum and you wanted yoghurt or seeds for breakfast, you could have either of these with a grated apple and a pinch of cinnamon, delicious. And no need for any other fruit that day.

Even if you are not following the programme for weight loss, you're likely to lose a few pounds in the first 2 weeks and most of this is likely to be water weight. To prevent further weight loss in phase 3 you will need to increase both your protein and vegetable portions and keep the ratios the same, i.e. equal weights of each. Start by increasing your portions by 10g and work up or down from there.

A note on pulses and soy

Peanuts, peas, beans, lentils and chickpeas are all pulses. Because pulses contain anti-nutrients including lectins, saponins, and enzyme inhibitors, I've always advised against eating them. You've possibly heard the stories about violent illness caused by eating raw or under-cooked kidney beans[1] and that lima beans (butterbeans) contain cyanide. But my mind was changed when I signed up to study Roger Green's *Longevity Diet*. Roger is the founder and director of the *Academy of Healing Nutrition* in New York – now also running in London and Prague - and his curriculum combines ancient Eastern medicine with up to date research. We had hands-on cookery classes and learnt how to make herbal elixirs and tonics – it was as fascinating as it was fun.

Roger teaches that pulses, of which there are 1000s of edible varieties, have long been a staple in the human diet and, provided we cook them properly, they're a great source of fibre and vegetarian protein. To deactivate their toxins and make them more digestible: soak pulses overnight, then drain and rinse them before cooking. Bring them to a boil and add a strip of Kombu to the water. Kombu is a seaweed that improves the digestibility of beans by breaking down some of the enzymes that make them problematic for us. Boil the beans for 10 minute and then, for best results, follow with some long, slow cooking.

Generally speaking animal protein is superior to vegetarian protein but as mentioned before, soy is a high value protein, and when it's fermented, as in tempeh, miso or natto it is easily digested and positively good for us. Soy that's been made into sausages and other imitation meat or cheese substitutes, is highly processed and best avoided.

Full-fat makes us thinner

Why full-fat yoghurt? The fat keeps us going for longer without feeling hungry, and full-fat yoghurt contains less carbohydrate, which as we know is easily converted into sugar and stored as fat. If a low-fat yoghurt is set, rather than runny, it has some kind of starch added to it (even though there's nothing on the label). If you're used to low-fat yoghurt it's certainly going to feel very naughty to eat full-fat Greek-style yoghurt again. When the fat is skimmed off milk, the fat-soluble vitamins, including A and D, are also skimmed off. Full-fat yoghurt not only keeps us going longer, it gives us more nutrients too.

The dogma that a low-fat diet is a healthy diet has been so severely drummed into us that it can be challenging to overturn that belief. But a low-fat diet, especially when it's low-fat dairy, is not the answer for health or for weight-loss. A 2013 study in Scandinavia tracked the dairy intake and obesity rates of more than 1,500 middle-aged adults.[2] The ones who often ate butter, full-fat milk and cream, were thinner than those who chose the low-fat options. "Based on my own research and on the research of others, I believe high-fat dairy is less likely to contribute to obesity that low-fat dairy," said the author of the study, Dr. Sara Holmberg.

If you're following the programme for weight loss, you're better off eating more protein early in the day – fish, eggs or chicken (and vegetables), rather than yoghurt or seeds. In practice I normally advise people to steer clear of dairy until phase 3 because it is a problematic food for so many of us. It's often the case that it's only once we eliminate a food for a period of time before re-introducing it, that we realise how it's affecting us.

One of the upsides of keeping a food diary is to help you keep track of which breakfast keeps you going the best. Remember that when you start you may well feel hungry for the first couple of days. That's normal; it takes a little time to adjust to a new way of eating. When you feel hungry stretch out your stomach with water and ghrelin, the hunger hormone, goes away.

Breakfast – the most controversial meal of the day?

When we're in a healthy and balanced state, there's nothing wrong with skipping breakfast; in fact it's positively healthy to extend the overnight fast well into the next day. I used to believe that breakfast was optional for everyone. But I've come to understand that if we're out of balance and our internal clocks are out of sync, breakfast acts as a 'zeitgeber'. In other words, eating breakfast helps to restore our all-important internal rhythm. Once you're back in balance, and in the forever phase you can experiment with skipping breakfast, or any of the other meals, and see how you feel; listen to the feedback from your body and brain.

We know consuming protein early in the day kick starts the metabolism and gets the body burning fat. Australian researchers in 2018[3] found that eating protein at breakfast time reduced hunger and cravings later in the day; the people who had protein for breakfast were less hungry and found it easier to lose weight. And because we also understand about the leptin reset now, that makes sense.

Foods to Consider Excluding for the 14 days of Phase 2

Potentially problematic foods include:

Nightshade vegetables – aubergine, peppers, tomatoes (and potatoes, but you will be avoiding these anyway in phase 2).

Dairy - milk, cheese, yoghurt (and milk chocolate, but that's also out for now).

Sweet potato.

Gluten containing foods – wheat, rye and barley.

Joint pain and inflammation – try cutting out nightshade foods. When you reintroduce them in phase 3, try them one at a time, i.e. have peppers one day and aubergine another day, and see if they exacerbate symptoms. At the same time avoid dairy foods, be they cow, sheep or goat, strictly for the whole of phase 2 before reintroducing them. Occasionally eliminating nightshades helps with pain while sometimes it makes no difference. Some people find that sweet potato results in pain. Red meat is pro-inflammatory so cut down on meat and eat more fish instead.

Sinus or skin problems – avoid dairy strictly for the first 16 days (and see the candida section). (Sugar can also be a culprit because it increases inflammation).

Hay fever – this is connected to 'oral allergy syndrome'. Foods that cross-react with birch tree pollen include: apple, apricot, cherry, peach, pear and plum, kiwi, carrot, celery, almonds and hazelnuts. All those foods can be excluded from the diet apart from the apple. If apples give you an itchy mouth or throat, try grating them. Or even baking them, rather than eating them raw.

Digestive problems including bloating, constipation or diarrhoea – cut out both dairy and gluten foods for at least a month before testing by reintroducing them.

Low mood or anxiety – dairy and/or gluten could be the culprits – cut both out for a month before testing one at a time.

Low energy – as above – cutting out dairy and gluten for a month can have dramatic results.

Dairy foods for calcium?

We don't need dairy foods in our diet to supply calcium. We've been brainwashed into believing that dairy, such as milk, cheese and yoghurt is the only way of getting enough calcium for our bones, but this just isn't true. Many foods including soy, leafy greens and nuts and seeds provide calcium. This is not to say that dairy is necessarily bad for us but there are 2 potential problems with it, one is lactose and the other is casein.

- Lactose is milk sugar. Without the enzyme, lactase, we can't digest it – wind, bloating and diarrhoea can be symptoms of 'lactose intolerance'.
- Casein, the major protein in dairy (the other one is whey) shares some similarities with gluten: it's difficult to digest, it's allergenic and, like gluten, can also act as an opioid in our brain, which makes it addictive (see casein addiction below).
- Cheese contains more casein (protein), and less lactose (sugar), than milk.

Here's an interesting fact: both casein and gluten can be used to make glue. Swiss builders used to use casein glue to stick their chalets together. Do you remember making flour and water into glue as a child? The word gluten comes from the Latin for glue.

A story of casein addiction*: A young woman in her 30s came to see me – she was unable to lose weight and suffered with sinus problems, mouth ulcers, anxiety, 'terrible lows' and insomnia. She also suffered frequent bouts of diarrhoea. Her food diary included oats and skimmed milk for breakfast, and daily lattes and cheese. She had cravings for cheese, coffee and sugar. On asking how she'd feel about getting rid of dairy for 2 weeks her eyes welled up with tears. She bravely agreed and she cut it out completely. Three weeks later, as agreed, she tried some cheese. Within minutes she had violent stomach cramps and diarrhoea. She went back to her dairy-free regime – but tried cheese again twice, with the same results, before giving it up forever. She lost the weight she wanted to lose and she was sleeping deeply. Sinus infections and mouth ulcers were gone and best of all the anxiety and low mood had vanished too.* Neal D. Barnard's book, *The Cheese Trap: How Breaking a Surprising Addiction Will Help You Lose Weight, Gain Energy, and Get Healthy*[4] is a good read.

Once you've completed the 16-day reset, and you've been 100% free of dairy you can try testing it – the test just requires a few bites of cheese on an empty stomach. But you may well feel so much better that you're disinclined to experiment, and of course you don't have to do this.

Metabolic flexibility

If your main concern is weight loss, you're probably wondering how much weight you can lose in the first 16 days. That's a difficult question to answer because generally speaking the more weight there is to lose, the faster it comes off. Anywhere from 6 to 14 pounds (2.7-6.3kg) or more is normal, depending on your starting weight and your 'metabolic flexibility', see below. Over the duration of the 12-week programme, expect to lose an average of 2-4 pounds per week (0.9-1.8kg).

In clinic, although it doesn't often happen, I've seen people switch straight into fat-burning mode without any muscle loss at all in the first week. This usually happens when they weren't eating enough protein before they started the programme. That smooth transition is the result of 'metabolic flexibility'[5] which is the ability to easily switch between energy sources; the ability to do this is a sign of good health. But for everyone else, the fat burning commences within the first 2 weeks and no more muscle is lost. That is to say no more muscle is lost as long as walking or Pilates/Tai chi/yoga is the only exercise taken. It can be hard to keep the faith while your body switches into fat burning with temporarily lower energy and increased hunger for the first couple of days, but I've never known anyone not to make the switch.

1   Rodhouse, J. C., Haugh, C. A., Roberts, D. & Gilbert, R. J. 1990. Red kidney bean poisoning in the UK: an analysis of 50 suspected incidents between 1976 and 1989. Epidemiology and Infection, 105(03):485-491. Available: https://www.ncbi.nlm.nih.gov/pmc/articles/PMC2271815/ [Accessed 30 September 2018]

2   Holmberg, S. and Thelin, A. (2013). High dairy fat intake related to less central obesity: A male cohort study with 12 years' follow-up. Scandinavian Journal of Primary Health Care, 31(2):89-94. Available: https://www.tandfonline.com/doi/full/10.3109/02813432.2012.757070 [Accessed 30 September 2018].

3   Stringer, S. & Richardson, R. 2018. Is breakfast protein the secret to weight loss? [Online]. CSIRO. Available: https://www.csiro.au/en/News/News-releases/2018/Is-breakfast-protein-the-secret-to-weight-loss [Accessed 30 September 2018]. Baum, J. I., Gray, M. & Binns, A. 2015. Breakfasts Higher in Protein Increase Postprandial Energy Expenditure, Increase Fat Oxidation, and Reduce Hunger in Overweight Children from 8 to 12 Years of Age. Journal of Nutrition, 145(10) 2229-2235. Available: https://academic.oup.com/jn/article/145/10/2229/4590095 [Accessed 30 September 2018]

4   Barnard, N. and Burton, D. (2017). The cheese trap: How Breaking a Surprising Addiction Will Help You Lose Weight, Gain Energy, and Get Healthy. New York: Grand Central Life & Style.

5   Galgani, J. E., Moro, C. & Ravussin, E. 2008. Metabolic flexibility and insulin resistance. American Journal of Physiology - Endocrinology and Metabolism, 295(5) E1009-E1017. Available: https://www.physiology.org/doi/full/10.1152/ajpendo.90558.2008 [Accessed 30 September 2018]

3: Phase 3 – Burn

How to do it

IT'S DAY **17** and you're feeling great. You've got through the most challenging part of the programme and it's a triumph. You've already noticed improvements in energy, digestion and sleep. Your clothes are looser (too big even) and you're feeling brighter and more optimistic and enjoying the feeling of being back in control.

This phase is for 10 weeks, or if you are following the programme for weight loss, until you reach your target weight. You're continuing with the rules you've been following in phase 2: eating 3 meals a day, fasting for 5 hours or longer between each meal, finishing your meal by 9pm. It's a relaxed continuation of phase 2 but there are 2 important additions: olive oil and a weekly treat meal. While you might have felt like a social pariah for the past 16 days and have missed eating out with friends, now's the time to resume your social life.

Because you've been weighing out your meals for the last 2 weeks, you've got your eye in, you know what a portion looks like. And because oil has been reintroduced, you can eat out again without having to worry about whether or not your food's been cooked with oil. Stick to grilled fish, meat or chicken and vegetables, unless it's a treat meal of course. But even if it's not a treat meal, a glass of wine with dinner now and then is absolutely fine.

The oil with superfood status

If there were such things as super foods, olive oil would certainly be near the top of the list. It's full of polyphenols, plant antioxidants that are antimicrobial (bug killers) and anti-inflammatory, but are also beloved by our friendly microbes. There's nothing wrong with coconut oil, butter or ghee, and you can reintroduce them if you'd like to in the forever phase, but meantime olive oil is recommended for it's incredible health-giving properties. Other plant oils, including sunflower, canola and rape are best avoided altogether. People often ask if they can use avocado oil. Avocados and their oil would also be high on the super food list but pride of place goes to olive oil. Choose extra virgin olive oil because it's highest in polyphenols – cook with it and put it on your salads.

If you're reading this before you've started the programme, it's unlikely that the idea of salad dressing or vinaigrette would sound too exciting. But you'll be surprised how good it tastes after 16 days without – although sometimes people say they no longer miss oil by the time they get to phase 3. But do add it back in, as well as the health benefits of the polyphenols, olive oil also improves the absorption of fat-soluble vitamins in salad and vegetables.

Much better to make your own dressing than buy it, and you can make several batches at a time. For 5 portions put 5 tablespoons of extra virgin olive oil into an empty jam jar, add a pinch of sea salt and a teaspoon of mustard (if you like it) and pepper and some herbs, then a garlic clove put through a crusher and 10-20 teaspoons of apple cider vinegar, depending on how much you like the taste, and shake it all up. No need to refrigerate it.

Use your body as a human lab

This is the time that you can experiment with reintroducing grains, such as rye bread if you'd like to. Make sure it's 100% rye (sourdough is best) with no added wheat. See how you feel – listen to your body. Does it make you feel more energetic or less? Do you notice any bloating? Do you feel hungrier than normal later that day, or the next day? If you don't notice any adverse effects, and you enjoy rye bread, feel free to have it now and again – up to 100g per day, and only with meals of course. If you make sure that's it's 100% rye bread with no added wheat, then you can test the effect that wheat has on you another day.

On your first treat meal, you could try introducing wheat or dairy – of course it's best to avoid something like pizza, which combines both foods, because you still won't know which one you might have a problem with. Say you're out for dinner and you'd like to test wheat, just say 'yes' to the bread basket for a change. If you're testing cheese, you could have some goat's cheese or feta as a starter. As above, with the rye bread, tune in to how you feel afterwards, and into the next day. Sometimes, when an offending food is tested, the first and almost instantaneous reaction can be either a blocked or runny nose. Other times there's no clue for 48 hours or so. But if you're feeling great and you've worked out that you're better off without these foods, don't bother to test them.

Even if wheat doesn't result in any obvious trouble, avoid getting into the habit of eating it regularly again – because of the leaky gut connection – but do include it in treat meals if you'd like to. Pasta, by the way, is made of durum wheat which is naturally lower in gluten than the wheat used to make bread, and is better tolerated.

Reintroducing exercise

Technically, as soon as you move into this phase you can start to exercise again. But save intense exercise for the end of the programme, because you're still not getting enough protein for muscle repair and rebuilding. And because the focus is still on reducing stress and reducing cortisol. Leisurely jogging is fine and you can include some weight training. But don't go too far; take it easy and avoid the temptation of using exercise to process feelings of anger or frustration. If you used exercise as a solution to process these feelings in the past, use your pen and pad, and infrared saunas instead.

Exercising before eating, caveman style, lowers inflammation and is positively good for us. For a quick and easy full-body mini-work out, do 20 press-ups and 40 squats before eating. And remember that 'sedentary death syndrome' i.e. sitting down for more than 40 minutes or so, is much worse and more pro-inflammatory than not working out. Do the squats and press ups and never mind what they say in the office. Pretty soon they'll want to be doing exactly what you're doing anyway.

The Weekly Treat Meal

It goes without saying that getting together with friends and family and eating and drinking is a great pleasure. A weekly treat meal is part of this programme; once a week (or sometimes twice a week when you've moved into the next phase) you break all the rules and have fun. You can have a starter and a main course and a dessert (with the sugar proviso – see the FAQs) and you can have wine, or even a cocktail. You can mix different proteins, have butter on your vegetables, take your time, and really enjoy it. Think steak and chips and béarnaise sauce, or a delicious creamy curry and a glass of wine or two.

Remember that there are 2 reasons for the treat meal; actually there are 3, but we'll cover the third reason in the next chapter:

1. Having lots of extra calories once a week re-stimulates fat-burning
2. Pleasure is good for us

If a low-calorie regime becomes a life-style, i.e. if it lasts longer than a few weeks, the metabolic rate drops in order to conserve energy; the body thinks it's running out of energy and it's going to do what it can to prevent us from starving to death. So once a week you take it by surprise and throw a lot of extra fuel into the furnace and the body ramps up the fat burning again.

You might well feel anxious about having the treat meal and breaking all the rules – but, from now on, breaking all the rules once a week *is* one of the rules. The weekly treat meal is one of the many reasons for this programme's success. If you're too 'good', and you don't do the feasting, you won't get the results that you're after. So stick to the rules and feast.

Just a word of warning on the treat meal. Although you can eat anything you like, and you've probably been fantasising about what you might feast on, your stomach will have shrunk. Don't cram too much in or you might not be able to sleep and will feel seriously rough the following day. It's more fun and more satisfying to have 2, 3 or 4 small plates and a couple of bites of dessert than 3 big portions you'll be unable to finish. The key is to listen to your body and stop when you're full. But that's just a suggestion.

Because the treat meal is so important and because it should be a pleasure, don't waste it. If you've got to go to a work lunch or dinner and you're not absolutely sure that there will be something on the menu that you'd like, eat before you go and enjoy the treat meal you deserve another day.

It's during the 10 weeks of this phase that eating in this way begins to feel less like a diet and more like a way of life. It becomes second nature to eat 3 meals a day, to fast 5 hours between meals and to resolutely avoid snacking, because it makes you feel so good. And of course you'll still be drinking lots of water too.

4: Phase 4 – Forever

FOR THE PAST 3 months you've been eating the foods that human beings evolved on, the foods which speak to your genes and which your body understands. And at the same time, you've been nurturing and feeding your old friends, the microbes. You have feasted and fasted your way to feeling, looking and being your best. You've discovered the foods which suit you and help to keep you energised, and you may well have discovered some that don't. You've reset your hormones, you've recovered your rhythm, you're happy in your skin.

Problems you'd previously seen as insurmountable, such as an inability to lose weight, skin problems, constant hunger, lack of energy, insomnia, aches and pains and cravings, have disappeared; they've simply vanished, and all because you've changed the way you eat. Say hello to the new you!

What are the changes ahead and how do you navigate the future? Now everything has been brought back into balance, you're ready for the advanced class. This is the time to experiment with missing meals, doing some intermittent fasting, having an extra treat meal here and there, and doing some occasional hard-core exercise. You might even try cold water swimming; challenge yourself. All those stressors are the ones that our genes understand, and they respond to stressors such as cold, heat, hunger and thirst by turning down inflammation and making us stronger and healthier still. Those stressors, the same ones our ancestors were routinely exposed to, may be temporarily unpleasant, but ultimately they make us feel better.

Throw out all the clothes that are too big – give them to charity shops, get them out of the house. If you don't do that you're giving a message to your subconscious that you'll need them again sometime. You might think of buying yourself something special, as a reward for succeeding, maybe something beautiful to wear. Something that gives you pleasure and makes you feel proud.

Cold Water Swimming?

Let me tell you about cold water swimming. My husband, through the winter months, would get up when it was still dark outside on gloomy London mornings, and head off for the Serpentine, a lake in Hyde Park. And there he would swim – the water temperature was between -1°C (30°F) and 12°C (53.6°F). Cold. And I would lie in bed thinking 'what is the matter with him?' But one day he persuaded me to come with him – 'just once, just to see what it's like' he said. Feeling sick at the thought of it, we set off for the park and I ventured into the icy water. It was one of those perfect winter mornings – the dawn was breaking, the sky was pink, and the water was glassy and still. I can't say that I enjoyed the freezing water, but the feeling afterwards, and the energy and elation that I felt, meant that I too was hooked. I'm now a seasoned cold water swimmer, and all the better for it.

Hormesis

You might remember reading that there are not 2, but 3 reasons for the weekly treat meal. The treat meal, as well as stimulating fat burning and giving us pleasure, is potentially a little poisonous. And a little poison is good for us too. This kind of poison is known as hormesis.[1] 'The right dose differentiates a poison from a remedy,' wrote the sixteenth-century physician Paracelsus. Too much poison is of course fatal but a little bit, giving ourselves a small shock, is strangely beneficial.

Most of the time we're eating fresh, natural and unrefined foods but once or twice a week we take our body by surprise and give it something 'bad' like French fries or a burger or a creamy dessert. I haven't found any research to support my theory that part of the benefit of the treat meal could be a hormetic response, but I suspect that it might be. Because eating those foods produces inflammation and the body is always keen to return to balance, to homeostasis. When our body is stressed, our cells produce more repairing proteins and more antioxidants – it's called an adaptive response. Intermittent periods of hunger and thirst, heat and cold, and intense exercise, are good for us.

Exercise

We heard in A Low Calorie Beginning earlier on about the beneficial effects of calorie-restriction on life extension. And that intermittent fasting re-sensitises our cells to insulin, which helps get us back into fat-burning mode. But what about exercise? Remember that exercise, especially fasted exercise, is not only vital for our physical and mental health but that it also makes our brains grow. Find a way to incorporate it into your life. The key is to find any kind of exercise that you enjoy and which leaves you feeling energised and satisfied.

CrossFit, or any kind of group training, is excellent; the group dynamic makes it more fun and adds a competitive edge to spur us on. Mix it up. Go for walks and bike rides in the great outdoors, and find a local group of outdoor exercisers. Get yourself a mini trampoline, a rebounder, and turn the music up. Challenge yourself with weights and resistance training and occasional cardio sessions. I recently came across 'Electrical Muscle Stimulation' (EMS) which delivers low-impact high-intensity strength training; it's a whole-body workout and, best of all, it's all over in 20 minutes.

This is the time to start experimenting. Not just with saunas, cold water swims and occasional intense exercise, but also with food. You're building on the discoveries you made in phase 3 – about what suits you and what makes you feel well, and which things are best avoided. You delight in eating fresh unprocessed natural food and you're always on the look-out for herbs and vegetables and fermented foods that you've never tried before. You hardly eat red meat anymore; your taste buds have changed so much that foods you may have viewed with disgust in the past, now taste delicious.

Post Holidays

If you overdo it over Christmas or Thanksgiving, or while you're on holiday, and you get blown off track, you know what to do about it; the power is in your hands. You can repeat the whole programme once a year, how about January when everyone's on the wagon anyway? If you've had a holiday of too much eating and drinking, just get back onto phase 3 again for a couple of weeks. Get strict about portion sizes, the 5-hour fast between meals, drinking lots of water and sticking to one type of protein per meal, and that will set you straight again. The programme is something you can always come back to when you need a reset.

The new normal

There's no going back now. This is your new normal and your new way of life. Now's the time to get the pen and paper out again and to write about how extraordinarily well you feel. Express your gratitude to your body for seizing its chance to return to health, to quell the inflammation, to help you lose weight and to bring all your hormones back into balance. You've broken the habits of a lifetime; you're back in charge, and it feels great.

1   Mattson, M. P. 2008. Hormesis Defined. Ageing Research Reviews, 7(1):1-7. Available: https://www.ncbi.nlm.nih.gov/pmc/articles/PMC2248601/ [Accessed 30 September 2018

FAQs

Anyone who should not follow this programme?
Small children, pregnant or lactating women, athletes.

Apple cider vinegar – I don't like it do I have to have it?
No, you don't have to, but you might find that as your taste buds change you'll feel differently about it. And remember that it can help with cravings, particularly for sugar.

Artificial sweeteners – are they okay?
No. Any kind of fake sweeteners, including the ones in fizzy drinks, are not only despised by our friendly microbes, but they also help to keep the sugar monster alive. And they make us hungry. Avoid them.

Butter and coconut or avocado oil – can I have these instead of olive oil?
Once you're in the forever phase those fats are fine but until then stick to olive oil; it's much better for you and full of plant antioxidants.

Breakfast – do I really need it?
Yes, at least until you get to the end of the programme. Once in the forever phase, you're back in balance and you can experiment with fasting between dinner and lunch, and skipping breakfast, but for now it's a vital part of the programme.

If you really can't face eating in the morning there is another way. Have 40-50g of plain, unflavoured whey protein isolate (not concentrate because it contains more milk sugar) shaken up with water. Get a shaker bottle with a metal ball to ensure a lump-free drink. And find a brand that doesn't contain emulsifiers; our microbes don't like them.

Cheating – what happens if I make a mistake or go off the rails?
Pat yourself down and get back on the programme and don't beat yourself up. Remember to read your 'reasons' first thing every morning. If you never wrote them down, this is the time to do it. Unless you're really clear about the reason you want to change something in your life - be it weight loss, or energy, or a gut-related problem, it all becomes academic. Remember that the first 16 days are sacrosanct – if you're serious about wanting that change you must find a way to get through them.

Cold – why do I feel cold?
Feeling cold is a common complaint in the first couple of weeks – it happens when we get rid of the carbs and tell our body it's got to use fat instead of sugar for energy. When we're too cold, or too hot, our body uses energy in the form of calories to heat us up or cool us down. Put more clothes on and reframe that feeling: I'm burning fat and it feels good, I love this feeling!

Eating out – how do I navigate it?
For the first 16 days avoid going out but if you have to go to a work event, plan your day so that you can eat before or after the event. And when you're out don't say 'no' to a drink, accept it and keep it in your hand but don't drink it. If you don't do that you might find you're bullied into drinking. If you must go to a restaurant choose plain grilled fish, chicken or meat – explain to the waiter that you are on a 'medical diet' and if any oil is added to your food you'll have to send it back.

Exercise – what's the best kind?
The best kind in the first 2 phases is walking, yoga and tai chi. No power walking and no panting – if you're out of breath you're doing

too much. After that try light resistance training and weights, avoid cardio until you've completed the 3 months (or are happy with where you are weight-wise if weight loss is your primary concern).

Food Diary – why do I need to keep one?
It's easy to kid ourselves about what we're eating and drinking. Write down the time and exactly what you had to eat (include the weights in the first 16 days). If you have any bothersome health symptoms, keep a note of those too and rate them from 1-10 with 1 being very slightly bothersome and 10 being almost unbearably bothersome. You may well find that some foods make symptoms worse and this is a helpful way to keep track, to see if a pattern emerges.

Food intolerances - how do I know which foods to avoid?
It's not until we completely eliminate a certain food, and then reintroduce it again after a period of at least 2 weeks, that we see how it might be affecting us. The results can be dramatic; it can be like unmasking the devil! Two of the most common problematic foods are wheat and dairy. Revisit the section in phase 3 for more.

Frozen vegetables – are they okay?
Yes, in fact frozen vegetables may contain more vitamins that the fresh ones because they're processed immediately after harvesting. Add 10% to the vegetable weight if your vegetables are frozen.

Fruit – why is there so little of it? Can I eat dried fruit?
We've read about apples and about why they're included. Berries are low in sugar while supplying lots of wonderful polyphenols/plant antioxidants. Mango is included as a source of fibre and beta carotene (and because in Ayurveda mangos are said to make us happy). Avoid dried fruit as it's too sweet and too easy to overeat. Keep all fruit to a minimum – it can mess up your blood sugar and make you hungry.

Gluten – what foods contain it?

Look out for anything made of flour, including wheat, rye and barley. Restaurants, especially French ones, often use flour in sauces, so if you'd still like to avoid it in phase 3, make sure you ask the waiter. Some restaurants even add flour to their chips/French fries because it makes them crunchy, so watch out.

Lemon juice – can I add it to my water?
Only with meals because you don't want anything interfering with the fat burning process – plain water only between meals. But lemon juice, or better still, apple cider vinegar, with meals is positively good for you.

Red meat – why can't I have it more than twice a week? What about processed meat?
Red meat is pro-inflammatory and what with all you've read about inflammation and the effects it has on our health, you probably know you want to do what you can to avoid it. It's fine to have red meat occasionally, but remember that fish and the oil it contains are highly anti-inflammatory, which makes fish a much better choice. If you don't like fish have chicken instead.

Eating red meat and processed meat, including ham, sausages and bacon, has been associated with cancer[1] and even mania[2] and if you're still in doubt, and still tempted by sausages or bacon, read Bee Wilson's excellent and comprehensive article for *The Guardian*.[3]

Seasoning – what can I use?
Herbs and spices including ginger, garlic, chilli, mustard powder, fresh horseradish, black pepper, Tamari (gluten free soy sauce) and Tabasco, make meals more interesting and can add to their nutritional value. And include fresh, dried or frozen herbs including tarragon, rosemary, thyme, oregano and basil. Avoid using herbs that have been sitting in the cupboard for months; they don't pack much of a punch when

they're old. Unless they're still aromatic get a new pot. Look at labels and avoid seasonings that list oil, sugar, molasses or 'flavouring' or anything unpronounceable, as an ingredient.

Self-sabotage – why do I keep caving myself in?

If you're clear about why you're following the programme and you're really serious about wanting to lose weight or improve your health but you can't get through the first 16 days, find help. Team up with a friend or better still find a professional coach, a cPNI practitioner or a Rapid Transformational Therapy (RTT) practitioner (see the Resources section) to help you get to the root of the problem.

Sugar – can I have it at my treat meal?

Lots of us find sugar almost impossible to resist. And a sweet tooth is a monster – the more sugar you feed it the more it demands; it can become insatiable. The great news is that if you cut off its supply and starve it for a few weeks, the sugar monster dies and you'll be free of its clutches forever. Sugar is a strong drug for some of us.

Of all the hundreds of people I've worked with on the programme, one sticks in my head as a failure. I had no idea at the time that sugar was potentially so addictive. The lady, let's call her Gilly, was moving into Phase 3 of the programme. I explained that she needed to add oil at this stage – to cook and to make salad dressing with olive oil. And we discussed the importance of the weekly treat meal. Phase 1 and 2 of the programme are low calorie and following a low-calorie regime for two weeks is positively good for us. But if we keep to a low-calorie regime for too long our body compensates (i.e. it prevents us from starving to death) by lowering the energy output. Having a treat meal, with lots of extra calories once a week stimulates fat burning and more weight loss.

Gilly asked me if she could have any sugar in her treat meal as she was a great fan of meringues. And, to my regret, I said 'Yes of course – you can have anything you like for your treat meal!' Having been sugar-free for more than 2 weeks, and liberated from the sugar monster, she had her meringues. But with that her sugar addiction was back with a vengeance and she was trapped again. So please be careful. If you felt seriously addicted to sugar before you started and you've got through the first 16 days without it, wait much longer before trying it again. Maybe 3 months. But maybe you'll need to avoid it for longer than that.

Remember that sugar gives us a quick energy hit but when it's broken down in the body it uses up micronutrients including chromium, magnesium, zinc, vitamin C and B vitamins – and those are the very things we need to produce energy. So ultimately sugar leaves us more exhausted.

Supplements – do I need to take them?

Ideally, we'd get everything we need from our diet. But unless we live on an organic farmstead with a couple of cows to fertilise the soil, and we're not exposed to any stress or pollution, I believe the answer is yes. Remember that as with everything else in life too much of anything is as bad as too little and the same goes for supplements. So keep it light. A multi is a good way to cover your bases – take a separate multi-mineral and a multi-vitamin unless you're taking a powdered multi. Calcium and iron are 2 minerals you don't want to overdo. Check the ingredients and avoid inorganic minerals which are harder to absorb – they are basically rocks. Minerals in inorganic forms, such as oxides and sulphates, may be less well absorbed than chelates, glycinate, citrate and malate forms.

- **Vitamin D** – 90% of the results I see in clinic come back low. As with everything else too much of any vitamin is as bad as too little. Get your levels checked. Here's a home test: http://www.vitamindtest.org.uk or ask your GP to test you. You can safely take 2000iu without getting tested but you may need much more than that.
- **Calcium** – many of us are worried about getting enough calcium if we stop eating dairy (see the section about phase 2). Many

cultures don't include any dairy in their diet and we don't need to supplement calcium as it's so widely available in vegetables, nuts and seeds. Don't supplement without professional advice.

- **Iron** – don't supplement unless you have low levels of iron in your blood and not without professional advice – too much iron is to be avoided.

- **Magnesium** – this is the mineral that I recommend the most because we burn through magnesium when we're under stress, and we don't get enough of it in our diet. Taking too much magnesium can result in diarrhoea but getting just the right amount can help with energy, muscle cramps and sleep. Start with about 400mg at bedtime and work up or down from there.

- **Betaine HCl** – this can help with protein digestion and mineral absorption. Look for a brand that also contains bitters and take 1-2 capsules with food if you feel bloated after eating and if you suffer with constipation. NB: Do not take this if you have stomach ulcers.

- **Chlorella** – see the 'bad breath' section in Troubleshooting.

Sweating – how can I get up a sweat without exercise and get the endorphins I'm used to if I can't exercise at the beginning of the programme?

It's odd to think that our biggest detox and immune organ is our skin, and that sweating can help to shift toxins such as heavy metals. Sitting in a sauna (far infrared is best) for 20-30 minutes not only helps to flush out toxins but it also improves circulation and generates feel-good endorphins. Three or more times a week would be perfect.

Vinegar – can I use balsamic or wine vinegar instead?
No. Balsamic is too sugary and it's best to stick to unfiltered organic apple cider vinegar. That's the vinegar that seems to have the most benefit. You can add it to water to drink with meals or put it in your salad but don't have it between meals.

Water – fizzy or flat? Hot or cold?

Flat's better for you than fizzy and it's much easier to drink. You can drink the water hot or cold but don't add lemon to it or anything else other than electrolyte drops. But remember the rat research that shows that fizzy water can make us hungrier? Drink your water flat, and save the fizzy, if you really want it, for when you're pretending you're drinking a G&T.

Weighing – how often should I weigh myself?
Don't obsess with the numbers on the scales. Unless you invest in a professional body composition analyser you won't know what the weight loss or weight gain signifies. It's common to gain 2-3 pounds after treat meals and that weight is water retention. Home scales are not particularly reliable. You're better off weighing yourself once a week. Or better still not at all. Once you're happy with your weight, the best way to keep tabs is by trying on your favourite jeans, or a favourite dress, once a week. It doesn't matter what the scales say as long as your favourite item of clothing fits you perfectly.

There's nothing worse than jumping on the scales first thing in the morning and seeing they've moved up a notch. That's a bad start to anyone's day and, psychologically speaking, means you're less likely to be 'good' for the rest of the day.

Weighing food portions – do I need to weigh them forever?
No. Weighing is all important for phase 2, but you'll be getting your eye in and pretty soon you'll be able to estimate the weights successfully. Test yourself in phase 3 by estimating the weight of the food and then checking by using the scales. Digital scales are the most accurate.

Weight maintenance – I don't need to lose weight but do want to improve my health? Will I lose weight?
It's inevitable that you will lose weight over the first 2 weeks – some of this will be fat, a little will be muscle and more than a little is likely to be water. Increase your portion sizes from the baseline weight

recommendations in phase 2 but keep the protein weight and the vegetable weights the same, e.g. 150g fish and 150g vegetables.

1   World Health Organization. 2015. Q&A on the carcinogenicity of the consumption of red meat and processed meat [Online]. WHO. Available: http://www.who.int/features/qa/cancer-red-meat/en/ [Accessed 30 September 2018].

2   Nilaweera, A. & Tantibanchachai, C. 2018. Beef Jerky and Other Processed Meats Associated with Manic Episodes [Online]. The Johns Hopkins University. Available: https://www.hopkinsmedicine.org/news/media/releases/beef_jerky_and_other_processed_meats_associated_with_manic_episodes [Accessed September 2018].

3   Wilson, B. 2018. Yes, bacon really is killing us [Online]. The Guardian. Available: https://www.theguardian.com/news/2018/mar/01/bacon-cancer-processed-meats-nitrates-nitrites-sausages [Accessed 30 September 2018].

Troubleshooting A-Z

Alcohol

See Cravings

Bad Breath

Most of us are paranoid about bad breath and it's true it can be bad when we're fasting and detoxing. Don't be tempted to chew gum; whether it's sweetened by sugar or fake sugar, it's going to have an impact on your blood sugar and might make you hungry too. Try chewing parsley after your meals instead. Chlorella can help to neutralise bad breath – take it with meals.

Candida

Candida is a yeast or fungus that's found in pretty much everyone's gut where it's a normal inhabitant, but commonly it can get out of hand. The linings of the intestine, and elsewhere besides, should be covered with a protective layer of microbes such as lactobacillus and bifidobacter bacteria. Bugs literally compete for space in our bodies – if we've got lots of the friendly microbes there is nowhere for the nasty ones, such as candida, to hide. Imagine a brick wall that's covered with moss. Provided the wall is covered with moss there's no space for any other plants to seed and grow. But if someone was to come along and pull out a handful of moss, anything that was floating about could dig itself in and seed there. And the same thing happens in our bodies. If our defences are down and we don't have good microbe coverage, the baddies find a place of their own and seize their chance to proliferate.

Some of the signs and symptoms of candida overgrowth include: thrush and athlete's foot, lack of energy and brain fog, skin problems, digestive symptoms including bloating and constipation or diarrhoea, chronic sinus problems, and cravings for sugar and carbohydrates.

Candida is ever more common for several reasons:

1. Antibiotics – these destroy the bacteria they were prescribed for but they also decimate our good gut microbes

2. We eat too many carbs and sugar which fuel bugs like candida, allowing them to grow and to displace our friendly microbes

3. Stress – our friendly microbes are not resilient (unlike the baddies); they don't like stress, they don't like parties or loud music or too much alcohol or not enough sleep. Knocking out the friendly bugs allows candida to proliferate

You've probably heard of the gut-brain connection. When bugs like candida are demanding sugar (their favourite food) the brain is sent looking for it. Even though consciously we're thinking, 'No, I don't want to eat sugar, it's no good for my diet and it'll make me wrinkly' the bugs are noisy and persistent and often win out.

So how to get rid of candida? As clinicians, we used to recommend a totally fruit, sugar and yeast-free diet for 3 months or so. This was not only very difficult and boring but it didn't work very well either. Candida is quite a wily bug and if sugar is restricted it will find something else to dine on. Garlic, cinnamon and caprylic acid, as well as plant tannin supplements, all show powerful anti-fungal properties – it's best to work with a practitioner to help you get rid of it.

Wang, Y. 2015. Looking into Candida albicans infection, host response, and antifungal strategies. Virulence, 6, 307-308.
Available: *https://www.ncbi.nlm.nih.gov/pmc/articles/PMC4601349/*

Cellulite

Two things can help you get rid of this pesky problem: skin brushing and trampolining. Get yourself a natural bristle body brush and use it before your shower in the morning. Brush upwards towards your heart and use circular movements on your belly and bottom. Rebounding, jumping on a mini trampoline, is not only energising and fun but it also stimulates the flow of lymph which can help to shift cellulite.

Constipation

A common and undesirable side-effect of changing dietary habits, and in particular eliminating wheat, is constipation. The most reliable set of bowels can turn stubborn when wheat is removed from the diet. This is partly because you're missing out on the fibre supplied by whole grains. But because wheat can act as an opioid for some of us (and we know that opioids like morphine are constipating) it can have the opposite effect; once we get rid of wheat then we become more regular.

Regular bowel movements are vital, not just for weight loss but for overall health. The liver goes to a lot of trouble to wrap up toxins with bile from the gall bladder so that they're ready to be excreted. But if the toxins are hanging around too long because we're constipated these little packets get undone, the toxins get back into circulation and the liver has to do its work all over again. Other knock-on effects of constipation include slower weight loss, bad breath and an unpleasant taste in the mouth. So if you're drinking lots of water and following all the rules but everything's seized up, these things can help:

1. **Magnesium** works as a laxative by drawing water from the body into the colon and it also helps everything in the body to relax. Taking just the right amount can keep things ticking over but taking too much can result in diarrhoea. There isn't a universal dose which works for everyone. Start with about 400mg magnesium citrate (in a powder or tablet, it doesn't matter which) and work up or down from there – it's best taken at night as it can also help with sleep

2. **Cascara compound** – the old naturopaths have been using cascara along with other herbs like barberry, rhubarb root, bayberry, wild yam, fennel, cayenne pepper and ginger successfully for decades. It's a good idea to do a bowel cleanse for several months if the constipation has been going on for some time and has become 'normal' for you. You can take 1-3 capsules per meal or take 4 or 5 capsules after dinner in the evening

3. **Probiotics** – the friendly microbes that are normal gut inhabitants can help with constipation in several ways. They add bulk to the stool, meaning it's easier to pass. In fact about ¾ of the weight of a normal stool is the dead bodies of the good bacteria. They also produce substances which provide energy for the digestive tract and the liver. They can also hydrate the stool, making it easier to pass. One particular microbe, L. casei (Rosell-215) which is one of the most extensively studied probiotic strains, increases the number of bifidobacteria. Bifidobacter are some of the main inhabitants of the large intestine and can help to improve regularity

4. **Walking** – the benefits of simply walking just can't be overestimated and a sedentary lifestyle is a sure-fire way to slow down the gut, so get those boots on and walk, even just 10-15 minutes, before each meal

5. **Dairy** – dairy foods can also encourage constipation so try cutting it out for at least 2 weeks and see if that helps

6. **Psyllium (pronounced sillium) husks** can get things moving again – try taking 2 teaspoons (10g) with a big glass of water, about ½ litre, 30 minutes before one of your daily meals

Cravings

Kudzu is a herb that's been long used by the Chinese to counter cravings for alcohol and sugar. Scientists studied the effect of the herb, kudzu, on alcoholic hamsters; Golden Syrian hamsters apparently prefer alcohol to water but when given kudzu they naturally began to drink more water. It seems to work in the same way for us too. Other studies have suggested it works not only to suppress sugar cravings but also to suppress appetite and some practitioners have found that it even helps to lessen menopausal hot flushes. If your cravings are more for salty foods than sweet, e.g. cheese – try a pinch of sea salt on your tongue.

Penetar, D. M., Toto, L. H., Lee, D. Y. W. & Lukas, S. E. 2015. A Single Dose of Kudzu Extract Reduces Alcohol Consumption in a Binge Drinking Paradigm. Drug and alcohol dependence, 153, 194-200. Available: https://www. ncbi.nlm.nih.gov/pmc/articles/PMC4510012/ [Accessed 30 September 2018]

Hunger

Although you'll probably be eating less than you were before you started the programme you should find that after 2-3 days of adjustment, you are no longer hungry. You're not hungry because you've got lower insulin levels. If you do feel hungry between meals (and you're drinking enough water) cut out fruit. If you have yoghurt for breakfast remember that the fruit is part of that meal and still needs to be included. But instead of berries or mango with the yoghurt have it with a grated apple and a pinch of cinnamon. That way you've had your apple and don't need any more fruit that day. Another strategy that helps is to have fruit *with* your meal rather than at the end; make protein the first and last bite of a meal.

Sometimes people really struggle initially with the 5-hour gap between meals because they're used to eating a high carb breakfast, and elevenses has become part of their life. Making new habits takes a bit of time and patience.

Check in with what you're really feeling – am I bored? Do I want a change of scene, like a quick walk? Remember that giving in to temptation, even to a cup of coffee, means that fat-burning stops and it will take longer to reach your goal.

Insomnia

That old wives' tale about an hour's sleep before midnight being worth 2 hours afterwards really does seem to be true. Aim to get to bed by 10pm. Sometimes despite our best intentions, and getting to bed early, we either can't drop off or can't stay asleep.

You can use a cannabis oil supplement (CBD) to help to relax you, and help you drop off – some of the best ones are lozenges which you allow to dissolve under your tongue. But if you're dropping off easily and waking at 2 or 3am, try taking extra magnesium, about 400mg, as magnesium glycinate, or bisglycinate, before you go to bed. An Epsom Salt bath can work wonders – add 3-4 big cups of it to a hot bath and soak for 10 minutes or longer before you go to bed.

Irregular Periods

This programme, because it rebalances your hormones, works to restore regular periods. But you might find that they jump about a bit for the first 3 months, popping up unexpectedly early or late, and this is a normal part of the process. If you have suffered with PMT/PMS that's likely to become a thing of the past. But while you're getting back into balance, try taking magnesium and vitamin B6 with meals, and starflower or evening primrose oil with dinner in the evening (and see the section on Resetting your Rhythm).

Muscle cramps

Muscle cramps are a sign that your body is short of magnesium and short of energy. We all have different requirements for this mineral depending on our diet and how much stress we're under or how much exercise we're doing. We need calcium for our muscles to contract and magnesium to allow them to relax. Try taking 400-600mg magnesium a day in divided doses – 100-200mg with food. And have an Epsom salt bath at night; the magnesium is soaked up by the skin.

Responsibility

Follow the programme with a friend, or better still find a coach you like. As with a friend, you need to know that the coach is on your side, and if you email with a question or a plea for help you'll get the help that you need.

Temptation

Take it one day at a time. Practice saying 'For today, I'm going to be saint-like. I don't know how I'll do tomorrow but for today, I am going to stick 100% with the rules'. Avoid saying 'no' to yourself because that makes us rebellious. And give yourself permission and say '*I might have that, but first I'm going to drink ½ litre water. Then I'm going to work out what I'm feeling*'. It might sound silly but get your pen and paper out (pen and paper seems to be more effective the typing) and get writing. Putting a little space between you and the temptation is often all it takes to get you through.

Weekends

If you're an early bird and naturally wake early on weekends too, you can skip this bit. But if you love lying in until 10 or 11, don't put your alarm on. How do you navigate 3 meals and 5 hours between them in that case? The answer is to have 2 meals. Skip breakfast and have brunch instead – stick to the same portion as for lunch.

Weight loss plateau

Patronising though it sounds, a weight loss plateau is often simply the result of being a bit too relaxed about your diet. Picture this scenario: you've lost quite a bit of weight and you're fitting into clothes you haven't been able to wear for ages. And you're feeling pretty good about yourself. Say your starting weight was 80kg, your goal weight was 65kg and you currently weigh 70kg. So maybe you're, maybe even unconsciously, thinking – well I lost that 10kg and I can easily lose 5 more, anytime I like, I'll get strict again soon and it will drop off.

We human beings are complicated. Knowing that losing another few kilos is possible doesn't make it urgent. So this would be the time to revisit your reasons why you wanted to lose weight in the first place and what was in your mind when you set your target weight goal.

But of course there may be other reasons. If you're observing the rules strictly and once you're into phase 3 you're adding oil to each meal, you're still relatively low on calories. Because the spectre of starvation lies deep within our ancient DNA, the body goes to a lot of trouble to prevent us from starving to death. Two weeks or so on a low-calorie diet doesn't have much impact on our metabolic rate. But much more time than that and our metabolic rate drops to compensate for the lack of energy coming in and it gets harder to lose weight. And that's why the treat meal is so important. Having a lot of extra calories once a week re-stimulates the fat burning process.

Here are some questions to ask yourself if weight loss has stalled:

- Am I drinking enough water?
- Am I getting enough sleep?
- Am I fasting for 5 hours or longer with water only between meals?
- Am I having a proper treat meal once a week with lots of extra calories? Remember that if you're too 'good' your body will adapt by lowering your metabolic rate, making it harder to burn fat. Take your body by surprise once a week – the extra calories once a week are a vital part of the programme
- Am I starting each meal with a bite of protein?
- Am I weighing my food portions?
- Am I having a bowel movement at least once a day? (If not see Constipation in this section)

Two Case Studies
(names have been changed)

I'VE LOST COUNT of the number of people who feel hopeless and that nothing's ever worked. They've tried everything (except this programme) and this is their last-ditch attempt to lose weight. But I *know* that they will succeed, and I know that you will succeed; you will lose the weight you want to lose and you'll keep it off. I know you are going to be very happy and that makes me very happy too.

Michael was in his early 50s and feeling pretty fed-up. He wanted to lose weight and, almost equally importantly, he wanted to improve his energy levels which he rated 4/10. He used to play a lot of sport but work life had got in the way and he'd gradually stopped playing football and tennis and noticed the weight creeping up. He'd been overweight for twenty years and didn't really believe that he could ever lose it but decided he'd give it a go. He was fed up not only with his low energy but also with muscle pains. He said the food or drinks he'd find hardest to give up were coffee, alcohol and bread – luckily he didn't have a sweet tooth.

Of course he was carrying much too much weight but it was his visceral fat, the dangerous fat, that bothered both of us the most. Visceral fat is the fat inside the body around the organs including the liver, pancreas and intestines and too much of it increases the risk of heart disease, type 2 diabetes, strokes and other chronic diseases.

Michael wanted to delay starting until the beginning of July as he had a holiday and some family celebrations over the course of the next month. His starting weight was 147.4kg (just over 23 stone) and his target was 114.5kg (18 stone) so he wanted to lose about 32kg or 5 stone in all.

Starting weight

- Weight 147.4 kg
- Fat % 44.9
- Fat mass 66.3kg
- Visceral fat 27
- Metabolic age 68
- BMI 40.6 – which put him into the 'morbidly obese' category

5 weeks after beginning the programme, he'd lost 7.7 kg overall. He'd lost 9.1kg of fat and gained 1.36kg muscle

- Weight 139.7kg
- Fat % 41
- Fat mass 57.2 kg
- Visceral fat 24
- Metabolic age unchanged at 68
- BMI 38.5 – he was now classed as 'obese'

16 weeks later he'd lost a total of 31.8kg

- Weight 111.9kg (he was below his target weight)
- Fat % 28.5
- Fat mass 31.8kg
- Visceral fat 14 – the cut-off for visceral fat is 13 so Michael was very nearly within the healthy range
- Metabolic age 62
- BMI 30.8 – he was still in the 'obese' category

We met again at the end of January and despite Christmas in the middle by this stage he'd lost a total of 44.6 kg

- Weight 102.8 kg
- Fat % 24.3
- Fat mass 25kg
- Visceral fat 12 (hurrah he was now in the safe range!)
- Metabolic age 48
- BMI 28.3 (and hurrah for that too which meant he was no longer 'obese' just 'overweight'

We are still in touch and his new target weight is 92kg and I'm sure he will get there.

Penny was at the other end of the spectrum. She had 3 children, a son and twin daughters, and just couldn't shift the baby weight. She worked out in the gym but too many biscuits, cake and chocolate had crept into her diet; she was a grazer, and she was eating too much fruit as well. Fruit and fruit juice are touted as 'healthy' but actually these foods are thinly disguised sugar-monster feeders. It really is true – the more sugar we eat the more sugar we crave. The worst time of day for her sugar cravings were between 4-6pm, when she said she felt out of control. Her energy was okay but certainly less good than it had been before the children and she'd had enough of feeling bloated. Her other consideration was that she was 42 and wanted to get her weight under control in good time before the menopause started to affect her.

When she came to see me in March Penny weighed 57.6 kg (just over 9 stone) and her target was 52 kg (just over 8 stone) so she didn't have much to lose. We've been led to believe that it's harder to lose weight when we have less to lose. But Penny, and many others besides, have demonstrated that this just isn't the case. In fact, it can work the other way around (see the information on fat and inflammation for the explanation) which means it can be harder for someone who's more seriously overweight to lose it.

Starting weight in the middle of March

- Weight 57.6 kg
- Fat % 26.2
- Fat mass 15.1 kg
- Visceral fat 3
- Metabolic age 27 (My body composition scales are stubborn and will never say that someone is more than 15 years younger than they actually are – so Penny was already 'the youngest' she was going to be)
- BMI 21.2

Six weeks after starting Penny had lost 5kg:

- Weight 53.1 kg
- Fat % 19.1
- Fat mass 10.1 kg
- Visceral fat 2
- Metabolic age 27
- BMI 19.5

By the end of May, 11 weeks after she started the programme Penny weighed 51.8 kg – she had surpassed her goal:

- Weight 51.8 kg
- Fat % 16.2
- Fat mass 8.4 kg
- Visceral fat 2
- Metabolic age 27
- BMI 19

At the end of her first week Penny already noticed she had more energy, she was no longer bloated and the awful 4-6pm sugar cravings had completely gone. But a couple of weeks later, following her treat meal, which included bread and ice cream, she woke next morning decidedly bloated. Many of us react badly to wheat, with bloating being one of the common side effects, so Penny agreed she would avoid it at her next treat meal. Her next treat meal included steak and chips with some vegetables, followed by chocolate mousse and ice cream. She was fine the next morning.

.

RECIPES

Oil-Free Soup Recipe for Days 1 and 2

Makes 3 portions – double the amounts if you want to have it both days

Ingredients

½ kilo pumpkin/butternut squash

1-2 large onions

2 cloves garlic (smoked garlic is great if you can find it)

½ kilo courgette

4-5 generous handfuls spinach leaves

1 tbsp rosemary

Pink salt and ground pepper for flavouring

½-1 litre clear fresh vegetable or chicken stock/broth

Shallots or chives

1. Roughly chop onion and garlic. Add to deep saucepan over medium heat and fry for about 5 minutes. Add a splash of stock to the pan so nothing sticks

2. While the onion and garlic are frying, roughly chop the pumpkin/squash and add to the pan with the rosemary

3. Season well with salt and pepper. Add about 500ml stock, turn the heat down and simmer gently for 15 minutes or until the pumpkin/squash is cooked

4. Add the chopped courgette to the pan, stir well, add another 250ml of stock and simmer for 15 minutes until the courgettes are also cooked through

5. Add spinach leaves. Stir well adding a little more stock if needed

6. After 2 minutes the spinach will have wilted

7. Turn heat off and allow to cool slightly before blending it. Or just enjoy the soup as it is

8. Pour into a bowl and add chopped chives or shallots

Breakfast Recipes

Apple Seed Muesli

35g mixed sunflower and pumpkin seeds

1 apple

½ tsp cinnamon/cloves

Seasoning to taste – salt and pepper

1. Soak seeds in water overnight. Drain and puree in the morning. Or use ground seeds (health food shop)

2. Coarsely grate the apple

3. Mix the grated apple with the seeds and add cinnamon and seasoning

Seeds with Avocado and Tomato on Rye Toast

35g mixed ground sunflower and pumpkin seeds

80g avocado

20g tomato

Mash ground seeds with 80g avocado – spread on a slice of toasted rye bread (100% rye – no other grains or seeds) and top with 20g sliced tomato or other vegetables

Mushrooms and Seeds on Rye Toast (Courtesy of Rita Carmichael www.nutrimatters.co.uk)

1-2 mushrooms

Kale and courgette or any other vegetable to make up the vegetable weight to 100g

1 tbsp fresh chopped herbs e.g. coriander, parsley, rosemary, basil

Fennel seeds – just a few

Garlic, 1 small clove, crushed

30g mixed pumpkin and sunflower seeds

Small slice of 100% rye bread

4 tbsp water or vegetable stock

Chop the vegetables and herbs

1. Weigh out your seed mix and rinse well if using whole seeds – no need to rinse if you're using ground seeds

2. Put stock into a pan and heat to a simmer

3. Cook the vegetables in the stock, then throw in herbs; season to taste

4. Add some fennel seeds and crushed garlic, if liked

5. Add the seeds and cook until all ingredients are heated through – about 5 minutes

6. Meanwhile, toast the rye bread

7. Pile the vegetables on the toasted rye bread

Lunch/Dinner Recipes

Fish Cakes

130g smoked cod or haddock

130g cauliflower, celeriac and butternut, or other type of squash, cooked and pureed

Cayenne pepper

Seasoning – salt and pepper and chopped chives/dill/parsley

1. Cook the fish (grill, bake or dry fry) for 4-5 minutes on each side

2. Once cooked flake fish with a fork

3. Add the pureed vegetables and mix together

4. Make into patties and grill (phase 2) or lightly fry in olive oil (phase 3)

5. Garnish with dill/parsley

Provençale Fish

130g fish (any fish, e.g. tuna, cod or salmon)

130g vegetables: artichoke hearts (bottled in brine in phase 2, or olive oil in phase 3) button mushrooms, courgette, tomato and shallots

½ cup fresh liquid vegetable stock

1 tsp Provençal herbs

Salt and pepper

1 clove of garlic

Fresh thyme and rosemary

1. Rinse the fish under cold water and pat dry

2. Trim the veg – if the mushrooms are small leave them whole; cut the courgettes into pieces, thinly slice the artichokes and dice the tomato

3. Fry the shallots in a hot non-stick pan – add the rest of the veg and braise lightly. Then add the stock and simmer for 10 minutes – season with Provençal herbs, salt and pepper

4. Put garlic through a garlic press, mix with salt and rub into the fish

5. Dry fry the fish for 3-5 minutes on each side and season

Arrange the fish and veg on a plate and garnish with thyme and rosemary

Turkey or Chicken Breast and Vegetable Puree

130g turkey or chicken breast

130g vegetables (e.g. parsnip/cauliflower/celeriac)

½ cup of vegetable stock

Oregano and marjoram

Salt and black pepper

1. Clean and chop the vegetables, simmer in vegetable stock

2. Once cooked, puree the vegetables with seasoning and herbs – keep warm

3. Wash turkey/chicken breast fillet under cold water, pat dry and then pound it between 2 sheets of plastic wrap/greaseproof paper to an even ½ inch thickness

4. Braise in a hot non-stick pan and season. Serve on a bed of pureed vegetables and sprinkle with chopped chives

Herbed Chicken Breast

130g chicken breast

65g tomato and shallots (i.e. half a portion of vegetables)

2 tbsp chopped herbs, e.g. parsley and thyme

Paprika and salt and pepper

Oregano, basil and marjoram

1. Preheat oven to 180C

2. Dice tomato and chop shallot

3. Braise shallots, tomatoes and herbs in a hot pan and season to taste

4. Season the chicken, cut into strips and fry lightly

5. Add shallot mixture and continue to cook

6. Season with oregano, basil and marjoram

7. Sprinkle oregano, basil and marjoram over chicken

8. Bake in oven for 10 minutes

9. Serve with salad leaves to make up the vegetable weight to 130g

Spicy Mince (turkey, chicken, beef or lamb mince)

130g lean mince

130g vegetables

1 piece of fresh ginger (about a small thumb – remember that ginger is hot!)

1 chilli pepper (optional) or a couple of drops of Tabasco

1 garlic clove

40g chopped shallots, 4 olives (remember to include these in your vegetable weight)

1 cup vegetable sock

Fresh coriander

1. Dice and peel ginger and garlic and chop finely

2. Cut chilli pepper open length-ways to remove and discard seeds. Chop finely

3. Lightly fry/braise mince in non-stick pan for approx. 10 mins stirring constantly

4. Add shallots, garlic, ginger and chilli pepper and season with salt and pepper

5. Slice olives and add to the mince, along with vegetable stock. Simmer for another 10 mins

6. Garnish with coriander and any other herbs you happen to have to hand and serve with salad to make up the vegetable weight to 130g

Beany Balls

80g beans (dried weight) if using tinned beans double the weight, i.e. 160g

130g vegetables or salad

Nutmeg/cloves

Turmeric

Salt and pepper

Mixed herbs – whatever's available

Fresh chives, chopped

Kombu, 1 strip

1. Pre-heat oven to 180C

2. Soak the beans overnight in cold water (or use tinned beans which don't require soaking)

3. Drain, rinse and bring beans to the boil for 10 minutes – add strip of kombu to the water

4. Reduce heat and simmer for a good 30 minutes with mixed herbs

5. Once cooked, drain the beans and puree or mash them together with seasoning and spices

6. Make mixture into balls and heat for 10-15 mins in the oven or, in phase 3, lightly fry in olive oil

7. Remove balls from oven and roll in chopped chives

8. Serve with salad or vegetables

Jam Jar Herbs – useful for perking up a fish or chicken fillet

1. Half fill a jam jar with apple cider vinegar (phase 2) or virgin olive oil (phase 3 & 4)

2. Mince, chop or shred a big handful of a mixture of fresh herbs, e.g. basil, coriander, mint and parsley and add them to the jar

3. Put a clove of garlic through a garlic press into the jar

4. Add finely chopped chilli (if you like it)

5. Shake it all up and store in the fridge and add a teaspoon to grilled fish or chicken

Resources

Alliance for Natural Health: From their website: *The Alliance for Natural Health International is an internationally active non-governmental organisation promoting natural and sustainable approaches to healthcare worldwide. Our catch cry is 'love nature, live naturally'* https://anhinternational.org

cPNI and MB Practitioners in the UK:

Karina Athwal (Oxfordshire)
Clinical Psychoneuroimmunology (cPNI) & Nutritional Therapy, MB Coach
karina@higherhealthandhealing.co.uk
www.higherhealthandhealing.co.uk

Fleur Borrelli, Dip cPNI, BSc Nut Med (London)
Co-Director The In-Sync Diet Ltd
Clinical Psycho-neuro-immunologist, Nutritional Therapist, MB Coach.
07766883522
fleurborrelli.com/theinsyncdiet.com

Nicki Edgell (Brighton)
Clinical Psycho-neuro-immunologist, MB Coach and Natural Nutritionist
nicki@nutritionandhealing.co.uk
www.nutritionandhealing.co.uk

Emma Finn (London)
Health Kinesiology, Psychoneuroimmunology (PNI) and nutritional advice, MB Coach
http://www.kinesienergy.com
emma@kinesienergy.com

Gloria Parfitt (London)
cPNI, Nutritional Therapy, MB Coach
www.metabolic-balance.co.uk
www.haleclinic.com

Cookery

Cookery book – easy and delicious and these recipes work every time: *Low Carb Revolution, Comfort Eating for Good Health* Annie Bell, Kyle Books, London 2014

Cookery course – more than just a cookery course: The Longevity Diet, Academy Healing Nutrition (London, New York and Prague)
London https://www.londonahn.com
New York: https://www.academyhealingnutrition.com/longevity-diet/

Exercise

London: https://www.e-pulsive.co.uk electrical muscle stimulation – an intense, whole-body work-out in 20 minutes – perfect
New York: https://epulsefitness.com

Foods

Fermented foods (sauerkraut etc.)
Planet Organic
Wholefoods
http://www.red23.co.uk

Gluten-free restaurant in London – there are a few but this is the original and the best (and owned by my husband) and it's reasonably priced too: Riccardo's, 126 Fulham Road, London SW3 6HU https://www.riccardos-italian-restaurant.co.uk

Other

Infrared sauna, UK https://www.health-mate.co.uk

Infrared sauna, US https://healthmatesauna.com

Metabolic Balance: www.metabolic-balance.co.uk

Non-toxic cookware: Green Pan https://www.greenpan.co.uk

Rapid Transformational Therapy (RTT) https://www.rapidtransforma-tionaltherapy.com/whatisrtt/ Find a practitioner: https://findatherapist.marisapeer.com/FAT/index.php

Water filtration (reverse osmosis under-sink units)
www.puretechsystems.co.uk

References/Bibliography

An, R. and McCaffrey, J. (2016). Plain water consumption in relation to energy intake and diet quality among US adults, 2005-2012. *Journal of Human Nutrition and Dietetics*, 29(5), pp.624-632.

The Anaphylaxis Campaign. 2015. Oral Allergy Syndrome [Online].

Anderson, S. (2017). *The psychobiotic revolution*. Washington, D.C.: National Geographic Society.

Ans, A., Anjum, I., Satija, V., Inayat, A., Asghar, Z., Akram, I. and Shrestha, B. (2018). Neurohormonal Regulation of Appetite and its Relationship with Stress: A Mini Literature Review. *Cureus*.

Asghari, M., Ghobadi, E., Moloudizargari, M., Fallah, M. and Abdollahi, M. (2018). Does the use of melatonin overcome drug resistance in cancer chemotherapy? *Life Sciences*, 196, pp.143-155.

Banting, W. (1863). *Letter on corpulence*. London: Harrison.

Barnard, N. and Burton, D. (2017). *The cheese trap: How Breaking a Surprising Addiction Will Help You Lose Weight, Gain Energy, and Get Healthy*. New York: Grand Central Life & Style.

Basoli, V., Santaniello, S., Cruciani, S., Ginesu, G., Cossu, M., Delitala, A., Serra, P., Ventura, C. and Maioli, M. (2017). Melatonin and Vitamin D Interfere with the Adipogenic Fate of Adipose-Derived Stem Cells. *International Journal of Molecular Sciences*, 18(5), p.981.

Baum, J., Gray, M. and Binns, A. (2015). Breakfasts Higher in Protein Increase Postprandial Energy Expenditure, Increase Fat Oxidation, and Reduce Hunger in Overweight Children from 8 to 12 Years of Age. *The Journal of Nutrition*, 145(10), pp.2229-2235.

Bischoff, S., Barbara, G., Buurman, W., Ockhuizen, T., Schulzke, J., Serino, M., Tilg, H., Watson, A. and Wells, J. (2014). Intestinal permeability – a new target for disease prevention and therapy. *BMC Gastroenterology*, 14(1).

Blaser, M. (2014). *Missing microbes*. London: Oneworld Publications.

Bloomfield, S., Rook, G., Scott, E., Shanahan, F., Stanwell-Smith, R. and Turner, P. (2016). Time to abandon the hygiene hypothesis: new perspectives on allergic disease, the human microbiome, infectious disease prevention and the role of targeted hygiene. *Perspectives in Public Health*, 136(4), pp.213-224.

Bosma-den Boer, M., van Wetten, M. and Pruimboom, L. (2012). Chronic inflammatory diseases are stimulated by current lifestyle: how diet, stress levels and medication prevent our body from recovering. *Nutrition & Metabolism*, 9(1), p.32.

Briggs, A., Mizdrak, A. and Scarborough, P. (2013). A statin a day keeps the doctor away: comparative proverb assessment modelling study. *BMJ*, 347(dec17 2), pp.f7267-f7267.

Campos, M. (2017). Leaky gut: What is it, and what does it mean for you? [Online]. Harvard Health Publishing.

Cani, P. and de Vos, W. (2017). Next-Generation Beneficial Microbes: The Case of Akkermansia muciniphila. *Frontiers in Microbiology*, 8:1765

Casas, R. and Estruch, R. (2016). Dietary Patterns, Foods, Nutrients and Chronic Inflammatory Disorders. *Immunome Research*, 12(2).

Castro, R. 2016. Reactive hypoglycemia: What can I do? [Online]. Mayo Foundation for Medical Education and Research

Chen, L., Chen, R., Wang, H. and Liang, F. (2015). Mechanisms Linking Inflammation to Insulin Resistance. *International Journal of Endocrinology*, 2015, pp.1-9.

Clatici, V. G. et al 2017. Perceived Age and Life Style. The Specific Contributions of Seven Factors Involved in Health and Beauty. *Maedica*, 12(3)191-201.

Coelho, M., Oliveira, T. and Fernandes, R. (2013). State of the art paper Biochemistry of adipose tissue: an endocrine organ. *Archives of Medical Science*, 2, pp.191-200.

Collingham, L. 2011. The Taste of War: World War II and the Battle for Food, London, UK, Allen Lane

Cory, H., Passarelli, S., Szeto, J., Tamez, M. and Mattei, J. (2018). The Role of Polyphenols in Human Health and Food Systems: A Mini-Review. *Frontiers in Nutrition*, 5.

De Lange, C. 2016. In Sync: How to take control of your many body clocks [Online]. New Scientist.

de Luca, C. and Olefsky, J. (2007). Inflammation and insulin resistance. *FEBS Letters*, 582(1), pp.97-105.

Deloose, E. and Tack, J. (2016). Redefining the functional roles of the gastrointestinal migrating motor complex and motilin in small bacterial overgrowth and hunger signaling. *American Journal of Physiology-Gastrointestinal and Liver Physiology*, 310(4), pp.G228-G233.

DePoy, L., McClung, C. and Logan, R. (2017). Neural Mechanisms of Circadian Regulation of Natural and Drug Reward. *Neural Plasticity*, 2017, pp.1-14.

de Punder, K. and Pruimboom, L. (2015). Stress Induces Endotoxemia and Low-Grade Inflammation by Increasing Barrier Permeability. *Frontiers in Immunology*, 6.

Epel, E., Lapidus, R., McEwen, B. and Brownell, K. (2001). Stress may add bite to appetite in women: a laboratory study of stress-induced cortisol and eating behavior. *Psychoneuroendocrinology*, 26(1), pp.37-49.

Eweis, D., Abed, F. and Stiban, J. (2017). Carbon dioxide in carbonated beverages induces ghrelin release and increased food consumption in male rats: Implications on the onset of obesity. *Obesity Research & Clinical Practice*, 11(5), pp.534-543.

Fallah, A., Mohammad-Hasani, A. & Colagar, A. H. 2018. Zinc is an Essential Element for Male Fertility: A Review of Zn Roles in Men's Health, Germination, Sperm Quality, and Fertilization. *Journal of Reproduction & Infertility,* 19(2),pp.69-81.

Fasano, A. (2012). Intestinal Permeability and Its Regulation by Zonulin: Diagnostic and Therapeutic Implications. *Clinical Gastroenterology and Hepatology*, 10(10), pp.1096-1100.

Fasano, A., Flaherty, S. & Gannon, R. 2014. Gluten Freedom: The Nation's Leading Expert Offers the Essential Guide to a Healthy, Gluten-Free Lifestyle, Toronto, CA, John Wiley & Sons Canada, Limited.

Fournet, M., Bonté, F. and Desmoulière, A. (2018). Glycation Damage: A Possible Hub for Major Pathophysiological Disorders and Aging. *Aging and disease*, 9(5), p.880.

Fukunaka, A. and Fujitani, Y. (2018). Role of Zinc Homeostasis in the Pathogenesis of Diabetes and Obesity. *International Journal of Molecular Sciences*, 19(2), p.476.

Ferguson, D. 2016. Why is America turning away from Weight Watchers? Because it's hard work [Online]. The Guardian.

Galgani, J., Moro, C. and Ravussin, E. (2008). Metabolic flexibility and insulin resistance. *American Journal of Physiology-Endocrinology and Metabolism*, 295(5), pp.E1009-E1017.

Giugliano, D., Ceriello, A. and Esposito, K. (2006). The Effects of Diet on Inflammation. *Journal of the American College of Cardiology*, 48(4), pp.677-685.

Godoy, L., Rossignoli, M., Delfino-Pereira, P., Garcia-Cairasco, N. and de Lima Umeoka, E. (2018). A Comprehensive Overview on Stress Neurobiology: Basic Concepts and Clinical Implications. *Frontiers in Behavioral Neuroscience*, 12.

Grant, R. and Dixit, V. (2015). Adipose tissue as an immunological organ. *Obesity*, 23(3), pp.512-518.

Greenberg, J., Owen, D. and Geliebter, A. (2009). Decaffeinated Coffee and Glucose Metabolism in Young Men. *Diabetes Care*, 33(2), pp.278-280.

Hall, J. C., Rosbash, M. & Young, M. W. 2017. The 2017 Nobel Prize in Physiology or Medicine – Press release [Online]. Nobel Media AB.

Hansen, M., Jones, R. and Tocchini, K. (2017). Shinrin-Yoku (Forest Bathing) and Nature Therapy: A State-of-the-Art Review. *International Journal of Environmental Research and Public Health*, 14(8), p.851.

Higdon, J., Drake, V. J., Angelo, G. & Jump, D. B. 2014. Essential Fatty Acids [Online]. Linus Pauling Institute.

Holmberg, S. and Thelin, A. (2013). High dairy fat intake related to less central obesity: A male cohort study with 12 years' follow-up. *Scandinavian Journal of Primary Health Care*, 31(2), pp.89-94.

Holt-Lunstad, J. (2017). The Potential Public Health Relevance of Social Isolation and Loneliness: Prevalence, Epidemiology, and Risk Factors. *Public Policy & Aging Report*, 27(4), pp.127-130.

Hughes, K., Bellis, M., Hardcastle, K., Sethi, D., Butchart, A., Mikton, C., Jones, L. and Dunne, M. (2017). The effect of multiple adverse childhood experiences on health: a systematic review and meta-analysis. *The Lancet Public Health*, 2(8), pp.e356-e366.

Hurst, Y. and Fukuda, H. (2018). Effects of changes in eating speed on obesity in patients with diabetes: a secondary analysis of longitudinal health check-up data. *BMJ Open*, 8(1), p.e019589.

Jegatheesan, P. and De Bandt, J. (2017). Fructose and NAFLD: The Multifa ceted Aspects of Fructose Metabolism. *Nutrients*, 9(3), p.230.

Karhu, E., Forsgård, R., Alanko, L., Alfthan, H., Pussinen, P., Hämäläinen, E. and Korpela, R. (2017). Exercise and gastrointestinal symptoms: running-induced changes in intestinal permeability and markers of gastrointestinal function in asymptomatic and symptomatic runners. *European Journal of Applied Physiology*, 117(12), pp.2519-2526.

Knight, R. & Buhler, B. 2015. Follow Your Gut: The Enormous Impact of Tiny Microbes, New York, NY, Simon & Schuster: TED.

Kooijman, S., van den Berg, R., Ramkisoensing, A., Boon, M., Kuipers, E., Loef, M., Zonneveld, T., Lucassen, E., Sips, H., Chatzispyrou, I., Houtkooper, R., Meijer, J., Coomans, C., Biermasz, N. and Rensen, P. (2015). Prolonged daily light exposure increases body fat mass through attenuation of brown adipose tissue activity. *Proceedings of the National Academy of Sciences*, 112(21), pp.6748-6753.

Koutsos, A., Tuohy, K. and Lovegrove, J. (2015). Apples and Cardiovascular Health—Is the Gut Microbiota a Core Consideration? *Nutrients*, 7(6), pp.3959-3998.

Kruse, J. (2011). *Why is Oprah still Obese?* [online] Jackkruse.com.

Kruse, J., 2013. Epi-paleo Rx: The Prescription for Disease Reversal and Optimal Health. Optimized Life PLC

Lees, S. and Booth, F. (2004). Sedentary Death Syndrome. *Canadian Journal of Applied Physiology*, 29(4), pp.447-460.

Lima, G., Vianello, F., Corrêa, C., Campos, R. and Borguini, M. (2014). Polyphenols in Fruits and Vegetables and Its Effect on Human Health. *Food and Nutrition Sciences*, 05(11), pp.1065-1082.

Losurdo, G., Principi, M., Iannone, A., Amoruso, A., Ierardi, E., Leo, A. and Barone, M. (2018). Extra-intestinal manifestations of non-celiac gluten sensitivity: An expanding paradigm. *World Journal of Gastroenterology*, 24(14), pp.1521-1530.

Lustig, R. H. 2012. Fat Chance: Beating the Odds Against Sugar, Processed Food, Obesity, and Disease, New York, NY, Penguin Publishing Group

Mach, N. and Fuster-Botella, D. (2017). Endurance exercise and gut microbiota: A review. *Journal of Sport and Health Science*, 6(2), pp.179-197.

Magkos, F., Smith, G., Reeds, D., Okunade, A., Patterson, B. and Mittendorfer, B. (2013). One day of overfeeding impairs nocturnal glucose but not fatty acid homeostasis in overweight men. *Obesity*, 22(2), pp.435-440.

Majid, A. 2018. Mapped: the global epidemic of 'lifestyle' disease in charts [Online]. The Telegraph

Mandolesi, L., Polverino, A., Montuori, S., Foti, F., Ferraioli, G., Sorrentino, P. and Sorrentino, G. (2018). Effects of Physical Exercise on Cognitive Functioning and Wellbeing: Biological and Psychological Benefits. *Frontiers in Psychology*, 9.

Martinov, J., Krstić, M., Spasić, S., Miletić, S., Stefanović-Kojić, J., Nikolić-Kokić, A., Blagojević, D., Spasojević, I. and Spasić, M. (2017). Apple pectin-derived oligosaccharides produce carbon dioxide radical anion in Fenton reaction and prevent growth of Escherichia coli and Staphylococcus aureus. *Food Research International*, 100, pp.132-136.

Mattson, M. (2008). Hormesis defined. *Ageing Research Reviews*, 7(1), pp.1-7.

Methodist Hospital Houston. 2013. *Obesity makes fat cells act like they're infected* [Online]. Science Daily.

Minihane, A., Vinoy, S., Russell, W., Baka, A., Roche, H., Tuohy, K., Teeling, J., Blaak, E., Fenech, M., Vauzour, D., McArdle, H., Kremer, B., Sterkman, L., Vafeiadou, K., Benedetti, M., Williams, C. and Calder, P. (2015). Low-grade inflammation, diet composition and health: current research evidence and its translation. *British Journal of Nutrition*, 114(07), pp.999-1012.

Monda, V., Villano, I., Messina, A., Valenzano, A., Esposito, T., Moscatelli, F., Viggiano, A., Cibelli, G., Chieffi, S., Monda, M. and Messina, G. (2017). Exercise Modifies the Gut Microbiota with Positive Health Effects. *Oxidative Medicine and Cellular Longevity*, 2017, pp.1-8.

Monirujjaman, M. and Ferdouse, A. (2014). Metabolic and Physiological Roles of Branched-Chain Amino Acids. *Advances in Molecular Biology*, 2014, pp.1-6.

Mosdøl, A., Vist, G., Svendsen, C., Dirven, H., Lillegaard, I., Mathisen, G. and Husøy, T. (2018). Hypotheses and evidence related to intense sweeteners and effects on appetite and body weight changes: A scoping review of reviews. *PLOS ONE*, 13(7), p.e0199558.

Nesterenko, V. B., Nesterenko, A. V., Babenko, V. I., Yerkovich, T. V. & Babenko, I. V. 2004. Reducing the 137Cs-load in the organism of "Chernobyl" children with apple-pectin. Swiss Medical Weekly, 134(1-2) pp.24-27.

Nettleton, J., Reimer, R. and Shearer, J. (2016). Reshaping the gut microbiota: Impact of low calorie sweeteners and the link to insulin resistance? *Physiology & Behavior*, 164, pp.488-493.

National Health Service. 2017. Starchy foods and carbohydrates [Online].

Nicoll, R. and Henein, M. (2018). Caloric Restriction and Its Effect on Blood Pressure, Heart Rate Variability and Arterial Stiffness and Dilatation: A Review of the Evidence. *International Journal of Molecular Sciences*, 19(3), p.751.

Nilaweera, A. & Tantibanchachai, C. 2018. Beef Jerky and Other Processed Meats Associated with Manic Episodes [Online]. The Johns Hopkins University.

Ods.od.nih.gov. (2018). *Office of Dietary Supplements - Zinc*. [online].

Offer, A. 2008. British Manual Workers: From Producers to Consumers, c. 1950–2000. Contemporary British History, 22, 537-571.

Oike, H., Oishi, K. and Kobori, M. (2014). Nutrients, Clock Genes, and Chrononutrition. *Current Nutrition Reports*, 3(3), pp.204-212.

Ondrusova, K., Fatehi, M., Barr, A., Czarnecka, Z., Long, W., Suzuki, K., Campbell, S., Philippaert, K., Hubert, M., Tredget, E., Kwan, P., Touret, N., Wabitsch, M., Lee, K. and Light, P. (2017). Subcutaneous white adipocytes express a light sensitive signaling pathway mediated via a melanopsin/TRPC channel axis. *Scientific Reports*, 7.

Ott, B., Skurk, T., Hastreiter, L., Lagkouvardos, I., Fischer, S., Büttner, J., Kellerer, T., Clavel, T., Rychlik, M., Haller, D. and Hauner, H. (2017). Effect of caloric restriction on gut permeability, inflammation markers, and fecal microbiota in obese women. *Scientific Reports*, 7(1).

Ozdal, T., Sela, D., Xiao, J., Boyacioglu, D., Chen, F. and Capanoglu, E. (2016). The Reciprocal Interactions between Polyphenols and Gut Microbiota and Effects on Bioaccessibility. *Nutrients*, 8(2), p.78.

Pagano, E., Spinedi, E. and Gagliardino, J. (2016). White Adipose Tissue and Circadian Rhythm Dysfunctions in Obesity: Pathogenesis and Available Therapies. *Neuroendocrinology*, 104(4), pp.347-363.

Pantazopoulos, H., Gamble, K., Stork, O. and Amir, S. (2018). Circadian Rhythms in Regulation of Brain Processes and Role in Psychiatric Disorders. *Neural Plasticity*, 2018, pp.1-3.

Parretti, H., Aveyard, P., Blannin, A., Clifford, S., Coleman, S., Roalfe, A. and Daley, A. (2015). Efficacy of water preloading before main meals as a strategy for weight loss in primary care patients with obesity: RCT. *Obesity*, 23(9), pp.1785-1791.

Penetar, D., Toto, L., Lee, D. and Lukas, S. (2015). A single dose of kudzu extract reduces alcohol consumption in a binge drinking paradigm. *Drug and Alcohol Dependence*, 153, pp.194-200.

Pennebaker, J. W. 2004. Writing to Heal: A Guided Journal for Recovering from Trauma and Emotional Upheaval, New York, NY, New Harbinger Publications.

Perlmutter, D., 2013. Grain Brain, New York, NY, Little Brown & Company.

Peters, A., Kubera, B., Hubold, C. and Langemann, D. (2011). The Selfish Brain: Stress and Eating Behavior. *Frontiers in Neuroscience*, 5.

Peters, L. (1918). Diet and health, with key to the calories. Chicago, Reilly and Britton Co.

Phillips, C. (2017). Brain-Derived Neurotrophic Factor, Depression, and Physical Activity: Making the Neuroplastic Connection. *Neural Plasticity*, 2017, pp.1-17.

Pot, G., Almoosawi, S. and Stephen, A. (2016). Meal irregularity and cardiometabolic consequences: results from observational and intervention studies. *Proceedings of the Nutrition Society*, 75(04), pp.475-486.

Press Association. 2016. Official advice on low-fat diet and cholesterol is wrong, says health charity [Online]. The Guardian.

Pruimboom, L. and de Punder, K. (2015). The opioid effects of gluten exorphins: asymptomatic celiac disease. *Journal of Health, Population and Nutrition*, 33(24).

Pruimboom, L., Raison, C. and Muskiet, F. (2015). Physical Activity Protects the Human Brain against Metabolic Stress Induced by a Postprandial and Chronic Inflammation. *Behavioural Neurology*, 2015, pp.1-11.

Raison, C., Capuron, L. and Miller, A. (2006). Cytokines sing the blues: inflammation and the pathogenesis of depression. *Trends in Immunology*, 27(1), pp.24-31.

Redman, L., Smith, S., Burton, J., Martin, C., Il'yasova, D. and Ravussin, E. (2018). Metabolic Slowing and Reduced Oxidative Damage with Sustained Caloric Restriction Support the Rate of Living and Oxidative Damage Theories of Aging. *Cell Metabolism*, 27(4), pp.805-815.e4.

Reiter, R., Rosales-Corral, S., Tan, D., Acuna-Castroviejo, D., Qin, L., Yang, S. and Xu, K. (2017). Melatonin, a Full Service Anti-Cancer Agent: Inhibition of Initiation, Progression and Metastasis. *International Journal of Molecular Sciences*, 18(4), p.843.

Remely, M., Hippe, B., Geretschlaeger, I., Stegmayer, S., Hoefinger, I. and Haslberger, A. (2015). Increased gut microbiota diversity and abundance of Faecalibacterium prausnitzii and Akkermansia after fasting: a pilot study. *Wiener klinische Wochenschrift*, 127(9-10), pp.394-398.

Rettberg, J., Yao, J. and Brinton, R. (2014). Estrogen: A master regulator of bioenergetic systems in the brain and body. *Frontiers in Neuroendocrinology*, 35(1), pp.8-30.

Reunanen, J., Kainulainen, V., Huuskonen, L., Ottman, N., Belzer, C., Huhtinen, H., de Vos, W. and Satokari, R. (2015). Akkermansia muciniphila Adheres to Enterocytes and Strengthens the Integrity of the Epithelial Cell Layer. *Applied and Environmental Microbiology*, 81(11), pp.3655-3662.

Richards, B. J. & Richards, M. G. 2009. Mastering Leptin, Your Guide to Permanent Weight Loss and Optimum Health Minneapolis, MN, Wellness Resources Books

Rodhouse, J., Haugh, C., Roberts, D. and Gilbert, R. (1990). Red kidney bean poisoning in the UK: an analysis of 50 suspected incidents between 1976 and 1989. *Epidemiology and Infection*, 105(03), pp.485-491.

Rook G. A. W. The background to the Old Friend Hypothesis [Online].

Rudd, M. 2017. Body: Help! High-intensity training burnt off my muscles [Online]. The Sunday Times.

Rynders, C., Bergouignan, A., Kealey, E. and Bessesen, D. (2017). Ability to adjust nocturnal fat oxidation in response to overfeeding predicts 5-year weight gain in adults. *Obesity*, 25(5), pp.873-880.

Sarno, J. E. (2007). The Divided Mind: The Epidemic of Mindbody Disorders, New York, NY, HarperCollins.

Sarno, J. E. (2010). Healing Back Pain: The Mind-Body Connection, New York, NY, Grand Central Publishing.

Schaafsma, G. (2000). The Protein Digestibility–Corrected Amino Acid Score. *The Journal of Nutrition*, 130(7), pp.1865S-1867S.

Shechter, A. & Boivin, D. B. (2010). Sleep, Hormones, and Circadian Rhythms throughout the Menstrual Cycle in Healthy Women and Women with Premenstrual Dysphoric Disorder. *International Journal of Endocrinology*, 2010, 259345.

Schulz, L. C. 2010. The Dutch Hunger Winter and the developmental origins of health and disease. Proceedings of the National Academy of Sciences, 107, 16757-16758.

Sears, B. and Perry, M. (2015). The role of fatty acids in insulin resistance. *Lipids in Health and Disease*, 14(1).

Shechter, A. & Boivin, D. B. (2010). Sleep, Hormones, and Circadian Rhythms throughout the Menstrual Cycle in Healthy Women and Women with Premenstrual Dysphoric Disorder. *International Journal of Endocrinology*, 2010, 259345.

Shishehbor, F., Mansoori, A. and Shirani, F. (2017). Vinegar consumption can attenuate postprandial glucose and insulin responses; a systematic review and meta-analysis of clinical trials. *Diabetes Research and Clinical Practice*, 127, pp.1-9.

Shostak, A., Husse, J., Oster H. (2013). Circadian regulation of adipose function. *Adipocyte* 2(4) 201 206.

Siddiqui, F., Assam, P., de Souza, N., Sultana, R., Dalan, R. and Chan, E. (2018). Diabetes Control: Is Vinegar a Promising Candidate to Help Achieve Targets? *Journal of Evidence-Based Integrative Medicine*, 23, p.215658721775300.

Spector, T. 2015. *The Diet Myth - the real science behind what we eat.* London, Weidenfeld & Nicolson

Stern, J., Rutkowski, J. and Scherer, P. (2016). Adiponectin, Leptin, and Fatty Acids in the Maintenance of Metabolic Homeostasis through Adipose Tissue Crosstalk. *Cell Metabolism*, 23(5), pp.770-784.

Stringer, S. and Richardson, R. (2018). *Is breakfast protein the secret to weight loss? CSIRO.* [online]

Sturgeon, C. and Fasano, A. (2016). Zonulin, a regulator of epithelial and endothelial barrier functions, and its involvement in chronic inflammatory diseases. *Tissue Barriers*, 4(4), p.e1251384.

Sureda, A., Bibiloni, M., Julibert, A., Bouzas, C., Argelich, E., Llompart, I., Pons, A. and Tur, J. (2018). Adherence to the Mediterranean Diet and Inflammatory Markers. *Nutrients*, 10(1)62.

Swanson, G., Gorenz, A., Shaikh, M., Desai, V., Forsyth, C., Fogg, L., Burgess, H. and Keshavarzian, A. (2015). Decreased melatonin secretion is associated with increased intestinal permeability and marker of endotoxemia in alcoholics. *American Journal of Physiology-Gastrointestinal and Liver Physiology*, 308(12), pp.G1004-G1011.

van den Broeck, H., de Jong, H., Salentijn, E., Dekking, L., Bosch, D., Hamer, R., Gilissen, L., van der Meer, I. and Smulders, M. (2010). Presence of celiac disease epitopes in modern and old hexaploid wheat varieties: wheat breeding may have contributed to increased prevalence of celiac disease. *Theoretical and Applied Genetics*, 121(8), pp.1527-1539.

Volta, U., Bellentani, S., Bianchi, F., Brandi, G., De Franceschi, L., Miglioli, L., Granito, A., Balli, F. and Tiribelli, C. (2001). *Digestive Diseases and Sciences*, 46(7), pp.1500-1505.

Wang, T., Chang, W., Chiu, Y., Lee, C., Lin, K., Cheng, Y., Su, Y., Chung, H. and Huang, M. (2013). Relationships between changes in leptin and insulin resistance levels in obese individuals following weight loss. *The Kaohsiung Journal of Medical Sciences*, 29(8), pp.436-443.

Wang, X., Sparks, J., Bowyer, K. and Youngstedt, S. (2018). Influence of sleep restriction on weight loss outcomes associated with caloric restriction. *Sleep*, 41(5).

Wang, Y. (2015). Looking into Candida Albicans Infection, host response, and antifungal strategies. *Virulence*, 6(4), pp.307-308.

Watters, H. 2012. Exercise Alters Epigenetics [Online]. The Scientist.

Wierzbicka, J., Piotrowska, A. & Zmijewski, M. A. 2014. The renaissance of vitamin D. *Acta Biochimica Polonica*, 61(4), pp.679-686. Available:

Wilson, B. 2018. Yes, bacon really is killing us [Online]. The Guardian.

Wolverton, M. 2013. Living by the clock: The science of chronobiology [Online]. Medical Xpress.

World Health Organization. 2015. Q&A on the carcinogenicity of the consumption of red meat and processed meat [Online].

World Health Organization. 2018. Noncommunicable diseases [Online].

Index

C

D